The Horticulture Flow

Adapting to Natures Rhythms

Matt Dittman

Chapter 1: Understanding Natures Symphony

The Dance of Seasons

The rhythm of the seasons is a timeless symphony, each note played with precision, each movement flowing seamlessly into the next. This cyclical dance shapes the natural world in profound ways, dictating the lives of plants, animals, and humans alike. The seasons are not merely a backdrop to life but a driving force, an ever-present conductor orchestrating the growth, dormancy, and rebirth of ecosystems. Understanding and working with this rhythm is essential for anyone seeking to cultivate a harmonious and thriving garden.

Spring bursts forth with an energy that is almost palpable. As temperatures rise and daylight hours increase, nature awakens from its winter slumber. Dormant buds swell and burst into leaves and blossoms, seeds germinate, and wildlife emerges to reclaim its place in the landscape. This is a season of renewal and vulnerability. Plants are in a state of rapid growth, but they are also tender and susceptible to late frosts, pests, and erratic weather patterns. Gardeners must tread carefully during this time, balancing the eagerness to plant with the patience to wait for stable conditions. Soil preparation is key in spring, as the earth, softened by winter's moisture, becomes workable. It is a time to sow seeds, transplant young plants, and establish the foundation for the growing season ahead.

As spring transitions into summer, the landscape undergoes a dramatic transformation. Growth accelerates, and the garden reaches its peak of vitality. The days are long, and the sun's intensity fuels photosynthesis, driving plants to produce leaves, flowers, and fruits. This abundance is both a blessing and a challenge. Weeds thrive alongside cultivated plants, competing for nutrients, water, and sunlight. Pests and diseases can proliferate, their activity spurred by the warm temperatures. Water becomes a precious resource as evaporation rates soar. In this season, the gardener's role shifts from planting to maintaining. Mulching, watering, and strategic pruning become essential tasks to support the garden's health and productivity. Observing the needs of individual plants and responding with care ensures that the garden continues to flourish.

Autumn arrives with a sense of quiet urgency. The frenetic energy of summer gives way to a slower, more deliberate pace. Leaves change color and fall, fruits ripen, and plants begin to prepare for the coming dormancy. This is a season of harvest and reflection. The garden yields its bounty, offering the fruits of months of labor. It is also a time to prepare for the future. Collecting seeds, dividing perennials, and amending the soil with compost are all tasks that set the stage for the next growing season. Autumn is a reminder of the cyclical nature of life, a time to celebrate the successes of the past year while acknowledging the lessons learned.

Winter, often perceived as a time of stillness, is anything but dormant. Beneath the surface of the soil, roots continue to grow, microorganisms break down organic matter, and the garden quietly regenerates. Above ground, the landscape may appear barren, but this period of rest is vital for the health of the garden. It is a time to step back, observe, and plan. Pruning dormant trees and shrubs, protecting sensitive plants from frost, and maintaining tools and equipment are all tasks that keep the gardener connected to the rhythm of the seasons. Winter is also a time for introspection, a chance to dream and prepare for the burst of activity that spring will bring.

The transitions between seasons, often subtle and gradual, are just as important as the seasons themselves. These in-between times challenge gardeners to adapt and respond to changing conditions. A sudden warm spell in late winter can awaken plants prematurely, leaving them vulnerable to frost. A prolonged dry period in late summer can stress plants as they prepare for dormancy. These moments require attentiveness and flexibility, a willingness to observe and adjust as nature dictates.

The interplay of seasons creates a dynamic and ever-changing environment that rewards those who learn to work in harmony with it. Gardeners who embrace this dance find themselves not only cultivating plants but also nurturing a deeper connection to the natural world. Each season brings its unique challenges and opportunities, its own tempo and mood. By attuning to these rhythms, we align ourselves with the flow of life itself, becoming participants in the grand and eternal dance of the seasons.

Natural Cycles in Plant Life

Plants are deeply entwined with the natural cycles that govern their existence, a relationship shaped over millennia by the rhythms of the Earth. From germination to death, every stage of a plant's life is influenced by its internal biology and the external environment. These cycles are not just about survival but are also intricately linked to the ecosystems plants inhabit. Understanding the natural cycles in plant life is crucial for cultivating a thriving garden and nurturing a deeper connection to the world around us.

The cycle begins with the seed, a marvel of biological engineering. Encased within its protective shell lies the embryo of a future plant, along with the nutrients required to fuel its initial growth. Seeds are remarkable in their ability to remain dormant for extended periods, waiting patiently for the right conditions to awaken. This dormancy is an evolutionary adaptation, allowing seeds to survive harsh conditions and ensure germination occurs when the chances of survival are optimal. Temperature, moisture, light, and even chemical signals in the soil can all trigger the process. Some seeds require specific cues, such as exposure to cold temperatures or even passage through the digestive tract of an animal, to break dormancy. This ensures that germination aligns with the season or environment that offers the best opportunity for growth.

Once the seed germinates, the plant enters the vegetative stage, where its primary focus is on growth and resource accumulation. The seedling sends roots deep into the soil to anchor itself and absorb water and nutrients. Simultaneously, its stem and leaves reach upward, seeking sunlight to fuel photosynthesis. This stage is characterized by rapid cell division and elongation, as the plant establishes itself and builds the structures necessary for future development. The rate and direction of growth are influenced by environmental factors such as light, gravity, and the availability of resources. For example, plants exhibit phototropism, bending toward light to maximize photosynthetic efficiency. This adaptability ensures that they can respond to their environment and optimize their growth.

As the plant matures, it transitions to the reproductive stage, a period of remarkable transformation and energy investment. In flowering plants, this stage is marked by the development of flowers, which house the reproductive organs. Pollination, the transfer of pollen from male to female structures, is a critical step in the reproductive cycle. Plants have evolved a dazzling array of strategies to achieve this, from attracting insect pollinators with bright colors and sweet nectar to relying on wind or water to carry pollen. Once pollination occurs, fertilization follows, leading to the formation of seeds and fruit. This phase of the cycle is not only about perpetuating the species but also about creating opportunities for dispersal. Fruits and seeds are often designed to entice animals, who unknowingly assist in spreading the plant's progeny to new locations.

After reproduction, many plants enter a phase of senescence, where growth slows, and resources are redirected. Annual plants complete their life cycle within a single growing season, producing seeds before dying. Perennial plants, on the other hand, may enter a period of dormancy, shedding leaves and conserving energy to survive adverse conditions, such as winter or drought. This dormancy is not a sign of death but a strategic pause, allowing the plant to endure until conditions are favorable for growth to resume. The timing and duration of dormancy are influenced by environmental cues, such as changes in temperature and daylight. For deciduous trees, the brilliant display of autumn leaves is a prelude to this period of rest, as nutrients are reabsorbed and stored for the next growing season.

The final stage of the plant life cycle is death, a process that, paradoxically, is essential for the continuation of life. As plants die, they return nutrients to the soil, enriching it for future generations. Decomposing plant matter provides food for microorganisms, which play a vital role in breaking down organic material and releasing nutrients back into the ecosystem. This cycle of growth, reproduction, and decay ensures the sustainability of life and the health of the environment.

The interconnectedness of these natural cycles extends beyond individual plants. Ecosystems are shaped by the collective life cycles of all their inhabitants. For example, the flowering of plants provides food for pollinators, which in turn support the reproduction of other species. The timing of these events is often synchronized, creating a delicate balance that sustains biodiversity. When one element of this system is disrupted, the effects can ripple through the entire ecosystem.

For gardeners, understanding these cycles is more than just an academic exercise; it is a practical tool for creating resilient and productive gardens. By aligning gardening practices with the natural rhythms of plant life, we can work in harmony with nature rather than against it. Planting at the right time, allowing for natural dormancy, and returning organic matter to the soil are just a few ways to honor these cycles. This approach not only benefits the garden but also fosters a sense of stewardship and respect for the natural world.

The cycles of plant life are a testament to the ingenuity and adaptability of nature. Each stage, from seed to senescence, serves a purpose, contributing to the larger web of life. By observing and respecting these cycles, we gain insight into the intricate workings of the natural world and our place within it. In the garden, as in life, there is a time for every purpose, a rhythm that guides and sustains us all.

Reading Environmental Signals

The natural world is a complex and dynamic system, constantly sending out subtle signals about its state and needs. For a gardener, learning to read these environmental cues is an essential skill, one that fosters a deeper connection to the land and the plants nurtured within it. These signals are not always loud or obvious; they are woven into the patterns of light, temperature, moisture, and life that surround us. By paying attention to these indicators, it becomes possible to align gardening practices with nature's rhythms, creating a space where plants can thrive and ecosystems remain balanced.

Light is one of the most significant environmental signals for plants, dictating their growth patterns and life cycles. The length of daylight, known as photoperiod, influences processes like germination, flowering, and dormancy. Some plants, like lettuce and spinach, are triggered to flower by the longer days of summer, while others, such as chrysanthemums and poinsettias, bloom as daylight wanes in autumn. Observing how sunlight moves across the garden throughout the day and across the seasons is critical. A plant that thrives in full sun can become weak and leggy in the shade, while one that prefers shaded conditions may scorch in direct light. The changing angle of the sun throughout the year also affects microclimates within the garden, creating pockets of warmth or coolness that can be utilized to support diverse plantings.

Temperature is another foundational signal that influences plant behavior. Seeds often require specific temperature ranges to germinate, and plants rely on thermal cues to guide their growth and development. The first frost of autumn or the last frost of spring are milestones that mark transitions in the growing season, shaping what can be planted and when. Soil temperature, in particular, is a key factor that often goes unnoticed. Cool-season crops like peas and lettuce can be sown in cooler soils, while heat-loving plants such as tomatoes and peppers need the soil to warm significantly before they can thrive. Paying attention to these temperature thresholds can mean the difference between a thriving garden and one struggling to gain momentum.

Moisture levels in the soil and air are equally vital and provide critical information about a garden's health. Plants communicate their water needs through subtle changes in appearance: wilting leaves signal dehydration, while yellowing or browning may indicate overwatering or poor drainage. Soil texture and composition also play a pivotal role in water retention and drainage. Sandy soils dry out quickly, while clay soils can become waterlogged. Observing how water moves through the garden during and after rainfall can reveal areas prone to flooding or drought, guiding decisions about plant placement and irrigation strategies. Dew formation in the early morning can also serve as an indicator of local humidity levels, offering clues about the likelihood of fungal diseases or other moisture-related issues.

The soil itself is a rich source of environmental signals. Healthy soil teems with life, from earthworms and insects to microscopic bacteria and fungi, all of which contribute to its fertility and structure. A simple handful of soil can reveal a great deal: a rich, earthy smell suggests a thriving microbial community, while a sour or chemical odor may indicate imbalances or contamination. Cracks in the soil surface can point to compaction or drought stress, while a spongy, crumbly texture suggests good aeration and organic matter content. The color of the soil is another clue; darker soils often indicate higher levels of organic material, while pale or gray soils may lack nutrients or suffer from poor drainage. Testing the soil's pH and nutrient levels can provide additional insights, guiding amendments and plant choices to match the soil's natural characteristics.

Wildlife activity in and around the garden is another layer of environmental messaging. The presence or absence of pollinators like bees and butterflies can signal the health of the local ecosystem, as these creatures rely on diverse and abundant plant life to survive. Birds, too, can serve as indicators; their feeding and nesting habits often reflect the availability of food and shelter. On the other hand, an overabundance of certain pests may point to imbalances, such as a lack of natural predators or stressed plants that are more susceptible to attack. Observing these patterns can help in creating a garden that supports beneficial wildlife while minimizing harm from invasive or destructive species.

Even the wind carries signals that a gardener can decode. A prevailing breeze can influence plant growth, causing stems to grow sturdier or lean in a particular direction. Strong winds can dry out soil and plants, necessitating windbreaks or protective structures. The movement of air through the garden also affects pollination, as wind-pollinated plants like corn rely on air currents to transfer pollen between flowers. By understanding the wind's patterns, it becomes possible to design a garden that takes advantage of its benefits while mitigating its challenges.

Seasonal transitions bring their own set of environmental signals. The gradual shortening of days in late summer, the crispness of autumn air, or the swelling of buds in early spring all indicate shifts that influence what can be planted, harvested, or pruned. These transitions, though predictable, require close observation to act at the right moment. For instance, pruning too early in winter can expose plants to frost damage, while delaying too long in spring might interfere with flowering or fruiting.

Reading environmental signals is ultimately an act of attunement, a practice of stepping back and allowing nature to reveal its needs and intentions. It requires patience, curiosity, and a willingness to learn from the land itself. By cultivating this awareness, gardeners become not just caretakers of plants but participants in a larger ecological dialogue, responding to the cues that nature provides and working in harmony with the world's intricate designs. Through this partnership, the garden becomes more than a cultivated space—it transforms into a living, breathing reflection of the natural world's rhythms and wisdom.

Biological Rhythms in Gardens

Gardens are living, breathing ecosystems, and their vitality is deeply tied to the biological rhythms that govern the organisms within them. These rhythms, often subtle and intricate, are nature's way of orchestrating life processes in harmony with the environment. Plants, animals, microorganisms, and even the soil itself follow biological rhythms that are connected to time, light, seasons, and other external cues. Understanding these patterns allows gardeners to align their efforts with nature's timing, creating spaces that are not only productive and beautiful but also deeply connected to the natural world.

One of the most prominent biological rhythms in gardens is the circadian rhythm, a roughly 24-hour cycle that regulates the daily activities of plants and animals. In plants, this rhythm is manifest in processes such as photosynthesis, water absorption, and the opening and closing of stomata—tiny pores on the leaves that control gas exchange. During the day, plants actively photosynthesize, converting sunlight into energy while releasing oxygen into the atmosphere. At night, they shift their focus to other vital processes, such as repairing cells and redistributing nutrients. The timing of these activities is not random; it is finely tuned to the light and dark cycles of the day. Observing these patterns can help gardeners make informed decisions, such as watering plants early in the morning when stomata are open, allowing for efficient water uptake and minimal evaporation.

The behavior of pollinators and other garden wildlife is also influenced by circadian rhythms. Bees, for example, are most active during specific times of the day, often when flowers are producing the most nectar. Knowing the peak activity periods of pollinators can guide the placement and selection of plants to support their needs, enhancing pollination and boosting garden productivity. Similarly, nocturnal creatures such as moths and bats play crucial roles in pollination and pest control during the evening hours. Creating a garden that offers both daytime and nighttime resources ensures that these rhythms are supported and that a diverse range of organisms can thrive.

Beyond daily rhythms, gardens are shaped by longer biological cycles tied to the changing seasons. These seasonal rhythms influence when plants grow, bloom, set seed, and enter dormancy. Perennial plants, for instance, rely on seasonal cues like temperature and daylight length to determine when to break dormancy in spring and when to prepare for the cold months of winter. Annual plants complete their life cycles within a single growing season, timing their germination and flowering to coincide with favorable conditions. Understanding these seasonal patterns allows gardeners to plan activities such as planting, pruning, and harvesting to align with the natural cycles of their plants.

Dormancy is one of the most fascinating aspects of seasonal rhythms, particularly in temperate climates. Trees and shrubs, for example, shed their leaves in autumn as a way to conserve resources during the harsh winter months. Beneath the surface, however, they are far from inactive. Roots continue to grow slowly in the soil, and buds form in preparation for the burst of growth that will come in spring. Recognizing the importance of this resting phase is crucial for maintaining plant health. Overstimulating plants during dormancy, whether through excessive watering or fertilization, can disrupt these rhythms and weaken their resilience.

Biological rhythms also extend to the microscopic life within the soil, which is the foundation of any healthy garden. The activity of soil microorganisms follows natural cycles that are influenced by factors such as temperature, moisture, and the availability of organic matter. In warmer months, microbial activity peaks as bacteria and fungi break down organic material, releasing nutrients that plants can absorb. During colder periods, this activity slows, but it does not cease entirely. Certain fungi, for instance, form symbiotic relationships with plant roots, helping them access nutrients even in challenging conditions. Encouraging these natural rhythms through practices like seasonal composting and minimal soil disturbance not only enhances fertility but also supports the intricate web of life beneath the garden's surface.

The interplay of biological rhythms extends to pest and disease cycles as well. Many pests have specific periods of activity that coincide with the life stages of their host plants. For example, caterpillars may hatch just as tender leaves emerge in spring, while aphids often reproduce rapidly during warm, humid weather. Understanding these patterns enables gardeners to anticipate and manage potential issues without resorting to harmful chemicals. Encouraging natural predators, such as ladybugs and birds, is one effective way to keep pest populations in check, as these predators follow their own biological rhythms that align with those of their prey.

Even water cycles in the garden are influenced by biological rhythms. Plants have specific times when they are most efficient at absorbing water, and this efficiency is often tied to their daily and seasonal cycles. Watering at the wrong time can lead to stress, disease, or wasted resources. Observing how plants respond to moisture and adjusting irrigation practices accordingly ensures that water is used effectively and sustainably.

Biological rhythms are not static; they are dynamic and responsive, shaped by both natural and human influences. Climate change, urbanization, and other factors can disrupt these rhythms, leading to mismatches between plants and their pollinators, shifts in pest populations, or changes in the timing of growth and reproduction. For gardeners, this underscores the importance of paying close attention to the signals from their gardens and adapting practices to support resilience. Planting native species, preserving habitat for wildlife, and maintaining healthy soil are all ways to nurture the natural rhythms of a garden.

The beauty of biological rhythms lies in their interconnectedness. Each cycle, whether it is the daily opening of a flower or the seasonal migration of a pollinator, contributes to the larger symphony of life within the garden. By observing and respecting these rhythms, gardeners become partners with nature, working in harmony to create spaces that are not only productive but also deeply attuned to the world's natural order. This partnership is a reminder that the garden is not a separate entity but a living, breathing part of the broader ecosystem, bound by the same rhythms that govern all life.

The Web of Life Interconnections

Every garden is a microcosm of the larger natural world, intricately woven with countless connections that sustain life. These interconnections, often invisible to the untrained eye, form a delicate web that binds together plants, animals, microorganisms, and even the non-living components of the environment. This web of life is not merely a metaphor; it is a tangible reality, a network of relationships that keeps ecosystems functioning and thriving. To truly understand a garden's potential, one must first appreciate the complexity and beauty of these interconnections.

At the heart of this web lies the relationship between plants and the soil. Far from being an inert medium, soil is alive with microorganisms, fungi, and insects, all of which play vital roles in supporting plant life. Mycorrhizal fungi, for instance, form symbiotic relationships with plant roots, extending their reach deep into the soil and increasing their ability to absorb water and nutrients. In return, the fungi receive carbohydrates produced by the plant through photosynthesis. This exchange is not limited to individual plants; underground fungal networks often connect multiple plants, allowing them to share resources and even communicate about threats, such as pest infestations. This hidden network, sometimes referred to as the "wood wide web," underscores the profound interdependence that exists below the surface.

Above ground, plants engage in equally complex interactions with their pollinators. Bees, butterflies, birds, and even bats play essential roles in transferring pollen from one flower to another, enabling reproduction. These relationships are often highly specialized; certain plants have evolved unique flowers that cater exclusively to specific pollinators. The shape, color, and scent of a flower are all signals designed to attract the right visitor. For example, tubular flowers with bright red hues are tailored to hummingbirds, while pale, night-blooming flowers often rely on moths. These partnerships are mutually beneficial, with pollinators receiving nectar or pollen as a food source in exchange for their services.

The interconnections do not stop at pollination. Plants also rely on animals for seed dispersal, a critical step in their life cycle. Birds, mammals, and even insects contribute to this process, often without realizing it. Some seeds are encased in fleshy, nutrient-rich fruits designed to entice animals. After consuming the fruit, the seeds are excreted in a new location, often with a ready supply of fertilizer to aid germination. Other seeds are equipped with hooks or barbs that latch onto fur or feathers, hitching a ride to distant areas. These strategies ensure genetic diversity and allow plants to colonize new environments, strengthening the resilience of ecosystems.

Predation and pest control are other facets of the web of life that are often overlooked but critical to a garden's balance. Predatory insects like ladybugs and lacewings feed on aphids and other pests, keeping their populations in check. Birds and small mammals also contribute, preying on insects and rodents that might otherwise damage crops. Encouraging these natural predators by providing habitat, such as hedgerows, nesting boxes, or water sources, can reduce the need for chemical interventions and promote a more balanced ecosystem. The presence of these predators is a clear indicator of a healthy, functioning web of life.

Decomposition is another vital process in the web, recycling nutrients and returning them to the soil. Fungi, bacteria, and invertebrates such as earthworms and beetles break down organic matter, from fallen leaves to dead animals, transforming it into humus. This nutrient-rich material enhances soil fertility and structure, creating a foundation for new plant growth. The act of decomposition links every organism in the garden, reminding us that even in death, life continues and contributes to the greater whole.

Water, too, is a connecting thread in this intricate web. It flows through the soil, is absorbed by plant roots, and evaporates into the atmosphere, sustaining life at every step. Water bodies like ponds or streams within or near a garden support aquatic plants and animals, which in turn influence terrestrial ecosystems. Frogs, for example, rely on water for breeding but spend much of their lives on land, where they feed on insects. The presence of water also attracts birds and mammals, creating opportunities for even more interactions. The movement of water through the garden is a reminder of the interconnectedness of all ecosystems, linking the local to the global in a continuous cycle. activity is inextricably linked to this web, for better or worse. When gardeners choose to work with nature rather than against it, they become active participants in this network, enhancing its resilience and vitality. Practices such as composting, planting native species, and creating habitats for wildlife strengthen the web of life by supporting the organisms that make it possible. Conversely, actions like overuse of pesticides or monoculture planting can disrupt these connections, leading to imbalances that ripple through the ecosystem.

The web of life is not static; it is dynamic and ever-changing, responding to shifts in climate, the introduction of new species, and other environmental factors. This adaptability is both a strength and a vulnerability. While ecosystems can recover from disturbances, the loss of key species or persistent disruptions can weaken the entire network. For gardeners, this means that every choice, from plant selection to soil management, carries weight, influencing not just individual plants but the entire community of life within the garden.

This web is both intricate and robust, a testament to nature's ability to create order and balance from complexity. Each thread, whether it is a fungal network underground, a pollinator's flight path, or the cycle of nutrients through decomposition, is vital to the whole. By understanding and respecting these interconnections, gardeners can create spaces that are not only productive and beautiful but also deeply harmonious with the natural world. The garden becomes a living example of balance, a place where the interconnectedness of life is celebrated and sustained.

Chapter 2. Foundation of Flow Gardening

Principles of Natural Gardening

Natural gardening embraces the philosophy of working with nature rather than attempting to control it. This approach is rooted in respect for the ecological processes that sustain life, creating a harmonious balance between human intervention and the natural world. By observing and understanding the principles that govern ecosystems, gardeners can cultivate spaces that are not only productive and beautiful but also resilient and sustainable. These principles guide every decision, from soil preparation and plant selection to pest management and water use, ensuring that the garden thrives as part of the larger environment.

One of the foundational principles of natural gardening is the prioritization of soil health. The soil is the lifeblood of the garden, a complex ecosystem teeming with microorganisms, fungi, and organic matter. Rather than treating soil as a mere medium for holding plants, natural gardening recognizes it as a living entity that must be nurtured. Practices such as composting, mulching, and minimal tilling enrich the soil, fostering a vibrant community of organisms that break down organic matter and release nutrients. This process mimics the way nature replenishes the earth, creating fertile ground for plants to grow without the need for synthetic fertilizers. Healthy soil also improves water retention and drainage, reducing the risk of erosion and runoff while supporting robust root systems.

Another key principle is the use of native and adapted plants, which are naturally suited to the local climate, soil, and ecosystem. These plants have evolved over time to thrive in specific conditions, requiring less water, fertilizer, and pest control than non-native species. By incorporating native plants into the garden, gardeners not only reduce their ecological footprint but also create habitats for local wildlife, including pollinators, birds, and beneficial insects. This fosters biodiversity, ensuring that the garden becomes an integral part of the surrounding environment rather than an isolated space. In areas where native plants are unavailable or impractical, selecting species adapted to similar conditions can achieve similar benefits, provided they do not become invasive.

Diversity is another cornerstone of natural gardening. Monocultures—gardens dominated by a single plant species—are vulnerable to pests, diseases, and environmental stresses. A diverse garden, on the other hand, mimics natural ecosystems, where a variety of plants coexist in mutually beneficial relationships. Companion planting, where certain plants are grown together to support each other's growth, is a practical application of this principle. For example, planting marigolds among vegetables can deter pests, while legumes like peas and beans enrich the soil with nitrogen. This diversity extends to the structural levels of the garden as well, with a mix of ground covers, shrubs, and trees creating layers that provide shelter and resources for different organisms. Such complexity enhances the garden's resilience, allowing it to recover more quickly from disturbances.

The principle of minimal intervention is central to natural gardening. Instead of imposing rigid control over the garden, natural gardeners observe and respond to its needs, allowing ecological processes to unfold. This approach encourages patience and adaptability, recognizing that nature often knows best. For instance, rather than eradicating all weeds, gardeners might identify those that play a beneficial role, such as attracting pollinators or improving soil structure. Similarly, pests are not seen as enemies to be eliminated but as part of the food web, with natural predators and healthy plant communities keeping their populations in check. By stepping back and allowing the garden to find its equilibrium, gardeners create a space that is less labor-intensive and more self-sustaining.

Water conservation is another guiding principle, particularly in regions where water is a scarce resource. Natural gardening emphasizes efficient irrigation methods, such as drip systems or soaker hoses, which deliver water directly to the roots where it is needed most. Collecting rainwater in barrels or designing the garden to capture and retain rainfall reduces reliance on municipal water supplies. Mulching and planting drought-tolerant species further decrease water usage by minimizing evaporation and maintaining soil moisture. These practices not only save water but also create gardens that can endure periods of drought without significant stress.

Respect for the seasons and their rhythms is integral to natural gardening. Each season brings unique opportunities and challenges, from planting and growth in spring to harvesting and preparation in autumn. Natural gardeners align their activities with these cycles, taking cues from the changing environment. For example, pruning is done during dormancy to minimize stress on plants, while planting is timed to coincide with optimal soil and weather conditions. This seasonal awareness ensures that the garden remains in sync with nature, avoiding unnecessary disruptions to its balance.

The principle of closing the loop—recycling and reusing resources within the garden—further exemplifies the philosophy of natural gardening. Organic waste, such as kitchen scraps, grass clippings, and fallen leaves, is composted and returned to the soil, completing the cycle of nutrients. Rainwater is harvested and reused, and plant materials are repurposed for mulch or structures. By minimizing waste and making the most of available resources, gardeners reduce their impact on the environment and contribute to the sustainability of their gardens.

Ultimately, natural gardening is as much about a mindset as it is about specific practices. It requires stepping away from the notion of dominance over nature and embracing a role as a steward and participant in the ecosystem. This shift in perspective fosters a deeper appreciation for the interconnectedness of all life and the delicate balance that sustains it. A natural garden is not just a space for growing plants; it is a living, breathing community where every element, from the smallest insect to the tallest tree, plays a vital role.

By adhering to these principles, gardeners create spaces that are not only more sustainable but also more rewarding. The beauty of a natural garden lies not in its perfection but in its vitality, its ability to thrive as part of the larger tapestry of life. In these spaces, nature's wisdom becomes evident, offering lessons in patience, resilience, and the art of coexistence. Natural gardening is a celebration of life in all its forms, a reminder that by working with nature, we can create gardens that nourish both the earth and the soul.

Working With Not Against Nature

Nature operates with an inherent wisdom, a system of balance and resilience that has evolved over countless millennia. When we engage with it, especially in the context of gardening, the most effective and enduring approach is not to resist its processes but to collaborate with them. Working with nature instead of against it is a philosophy grounded in observation, patience, and respect. It requires understanding how ecosystems function and aligning human efforts with these natural processes rather than imposing artificial controls that disrupt the delicate equilibrium.

Every garden exists as part of a larger ecological context. It is not an isolated entity but a living fragment of the environment, influenced by the weather, soil, wildlife, and even the surrounding landscapes. Recognizing this interconnectedness is the starting point for creating a thriving garden. For example, the composition of the soil beneath your feet is not random; it reflects centuries of organic accumulation, mineral deposits, and microbial activity. Instead of stripping the soil of its natural qualities through chemical amendments or over-tilling, a collaborative approach might involve enriching it with compost, planting cover crops, or allowing microorganisms to flourish. These methods work in tandem with natural soil-building processes, ensuring long-term fertility and structure without depleting essential resources.

Water, a precious and often finite resource, is another area where cooperation with nature yields better results than resistance. In many traditional gardening practices, excessive watering can lead to runoff, soil erosion, and wasted resources. By observing how water naturally moves through the land—whether it pools in low areas, drains quickly in sandy soils, or lingers in dense clay—it becomes possible to adapt the garden's design to these conditions. Planting drought-tolerant species in arid regions or creating rain gardens in areas prone to flooding are examples of working with the land's natural hydrology. Mulching and preserving organic matter in the soil also help retain moisture, reducing the need for artificial irrigation and allowing plants to adapt to the rhythms of natural rainfall.

Pests and diseases are often viewed as adversaries to be eradicated, but this perspective can lead to an endless cycle of intervention. Nature, however, has its own methods for managing imbalances. Predatory insects, birds, and even certain fungi act as natural regulators, keeping pest populations in check. Instead of reaching for synthetic pesticides that can harm non-target species and disrupt ecosystems, a gardener might focus on attracting beneficial organisms. Planting diverse flowers to support pollinators, providing habitats for predatory insects, or fostering healthy soil where disease-resistant plants can thrive are all strategies that align with nature's own regulatory mechanisms. These practices not only reduce reliance on chemicals but also create a more resilient garden that can adapt to challenges over time.

Biodiversity is one of nature's most powerful tools for maintaining stability and productivity. In natural ecosystems, a wide range of plants, animals, and microorganisms coexist, each playing a specific role in the overall balance. Monoculture planting—growing a single crop over a large area—ignores this principle and often leads to vulnerabilities. A single pest infestation or disease outbreak can devastate an entire garden that lacks diversity. By contrast, incorporating a variety of plant species promotes a more stable environment. Each plant contributes something unique to the ecosystem, whether it's fixing nitrogen in the soil, attracting pollinators, or deterring pests. Companion planting, where certain plants are grown together for mutual benefit, exemplifies this principle. For instance, growing marigolds alongside tomatoes can deter nematodes, while planting basil nearby may improve the flavor and health of the tomatoes. This intentional diversity mirrors the complexity of natural systems and strengthens the garden's ability to withstand external pressures.

Seasonality is another aspect of nature that gardeners can embrace rather than fight. Every ecosystem operates on cycles of growth, dormancy, and renewal, and these rhythms are essential for sustaining life. Instead of forcing plants to grow out of season through artificial means, working with nature involves aligning gardening practices with these cycles. Planting cool-season crops when the soil is still warming in early spring or starting heat-loving vegetables only after the last frost ensures that the garden grows in harmony with the seasons. Allowing plants to rest during their dormant periods and preparing the soil for the next growing season are acts of patience that pay off in healthier, more productive gardens.

Even weeds, often seen as nuisances, have a role to play in this philosophy. Many weeds are pioneer species, designed to quickly colonize disturbed soil and protect it from erosion. They can indicate underlying soil conditions, such as compaction or nutrient imbalances, and some even bring nutrients up from deeper layers of the earth. While it's necessary to manage weeds to prevent them from overtaking desired plants, a natural approach involves understanding their purpose and removing them in ways that do not harm the soil. Hand-pulling, mulching, or using ground covers to outcompete weeds are strategies that respect the soil's integrity while maintaining control.

Wildlife presence in a garden, from insects to birds to mammals, is another testament to the interconnectedness of natural systems. Each creature contributes to the garden's health, whether by pollinating flowers, aerating the soil, or preying on pests. Encouraging wildlife often means creating a garden that mimics natural habitats—offering food, water, shelter, and nesting sites. A simple brush pile can provide refuge for small animals, while a shallow water feature might attract birds or amphibians. These elements not only enhance the garden's ecological function but also bring it to life, transforming it into a vibrant, dynamic space.

The philosophy of working with nature also extends to human effort. Gardening need not be a constant battle against the elements, requiring endless inputs of labor and resources. By observing and learning from nature, gardeners can reduce their workload while achieving better results. A no-till approach, for example, spares the backbreaking effort of turning soil while preserving its structure and microbial life. Similarly, choosing plants that are well-suited to the local climate eliminates the need for excessive fertilization or watering. This approach encourages gardeners to become stewards rather than controllers, participants in a system that is far greater and more intricate than any individual effort.

The rewards of working with nature are not merely practical but also deeply satisfying. A garden that thrives in harmony with its environment becomes a place of beauty and abundance, a reflection of the natural world's resilience and creativity. It invites a sense of wonder and gratitude, reminding us that we are not separate from nature but a part of it. By embracing this philosophy, gardening transforms from a task into a partnership, one in which the gardener and the land grow together, each enriched by the other.

Energy Conservation in Garden Design

Energy conservation in garden design is an approach that integrates thoughtful planning, efficient resource use, and an understanding of natural processes to create spaces that are both sustainable and functional. From the placement of plants to the use of materials and the management of resources, every decision contributes to the overall efficiency of a garden. Designing with energy conservation in mind not only reduces the environmental impact of a garden but also minimizes the labor and costs involved in its upkeep, making it an appealing and practical strategy for gardeners of all levels.

The orientation and layout of the garden are among the first considerations when designing for energy efficiency. Sunlight is a primary source of energy for plants, and its movement across the landscape determines which areas receive full sun, partial shade, or consistent shade throughout the day. By observing these patterns, gardeners can strategically place plants according to their light requirements. Crops and flowers that thrive in full sun should occupy the brightest spots, while shade-tolerant species can fill in areas that receive less direct light. This simple alignment with natural light patterns ensures that plants grow optimally without the need for supplementary lighting or excessive maintenance.

The placement of trees and shrubs also plays a crucial role in conserving energy within the garden and even for nearby structures. Deciduous trees planted on the southern or western side of a home provide shade during the summer months, reducing the need for air conditioning. In the winter, when these trees shed their leaves, sunlight can filter through, offering warmth and light. Similarly, evergreen trees and shrubs can act as windbreaks, shielding the garden and buildings from cold winds and lowering heating needs. These natural strategies leverage the energy-conserving potential of plants while enhancing the garden's microclimate.

Soil management is another aspect of garden design that can significantly impact energy efficiency. Healthy, well-structured soil retains moisture and nutrients more effectively, reducing the need for frequent watering and fertilization. Incorporating organic matter such as compost or leaf mulch improves the soil's ability to hold water, minimizing the need for irrigation. Raised beds or contour planting can help manage water flow, preventing runoff and ensuring that moisture is distributed evenly. By designing the garden with soil health in mind, gardeners can conserve both water and the energy required to transport and apply it.

Irrigation systems themselves are a key focus in energy-conscious garden design. Traditional overhead sprinklers often waste water through evaporation or by wetting areas that don't need it, such as pathways. More efficient systems like drip irrigation deliver water directly to the roots of plants, conserving both water and the energy needed to pump and distribute it. Timers and moisture sensors can further enhance efficiency, ensuring that water is only applied when and where it is needed. Collecting and using rainwater through barrels or cisterns reduces reliance on municipal water supplies and takes advantage of a free, natural resource. By integrating these systems into the garden's design, energy use is minimized, and plants are provided with consistent, efficient hydration.

The materials used in garden construction also affect energy conservation. Choosing locally sourced and sustainable materials reduces the energy costs associated with transportation and production. Stone, wood, and recycled materials can be incorporated into pathways, walls, and structures, blending functionality with environmental responsibility. Permeable surfaces, such as gravel or permeable pavers, allow water to infiltrate the soil rather than running off into storm drains, further contributing to the garden's energy efficiency. Designing with durability in mind ensures that these materials will last, reducing the need for frequent replacements and the energy involved in manufacturing new components.

Plant selection is another critical element in energy-efficient garden design. Native and drought-tolerant species require less water, fertilizer, and pest control, making them a natural choice for conservation-minded gardeners. These plants are adapted to the local climate and soil, thriving with minimal intervention. Grouping plants with similar water and sunlight needs into zones simplifies maintenance and reduces resource use. For example, placing water-intensive plants closer to a water source, while situating drought-tolerant species farther away, ensures that irrigation is applied efficiently.

Energy conservation extends beyond the plants and materials to the tools and techniques used in the garden. Manual tools, such as hand pruners and push mowers, require no fossil fuels and are quieter and more environmentally friendly than their motorized counterparts. When power tools are necessary, choosing energy-efficient models or those powered by renewable energy sources, such as solar-powered garden lights, complements the overall conservation strategy. Proper tool maintenance, such as sharpening blades and cleaning equipment, also ensures efficiency and prolongs their lifespan, reducing the energy required for replacements.

Designing for energy conservation also means considering the long-term sustainability of the garden. Perennial plants, which return year after year, require less energy to replant and establish than annuals. Edible landscaping, which combines ornamental and food-producing plants, maximizes the utility of the space while reducing the energy involved in transporting food from distant sources. Composting garden waste creates a closed-loop system, turning organic matter into nutrient-rich soil amendments that eliminate the need for synthetic fertilizers. These practices contribute to a self-sustaining garden that minimizes external inputs and energy use over time.

The role of wildlife in the garden ties directly into energy conservation as well. Pollinators, such as bees and butterflies, and natural predators, like birds and beneficial insects, perform critical functions that reduce the need for human intervention. Designing the garden to attract and support these creatures—through native plants, water sources, and shelter—strengthens the ecosystem's ability to regulate itself. This reduces the energy and resources required for tasks like pest control and pollination, creating a garden that works in harmony with its natural inhabitants.

Chapter 3: Seasonal Wisdom

Spring Awakening Techniques

As winter loosens its grip and the first whispers of spring stir the air, the garden begins to awaken from its long dormancy. This seasonal transition is one of nature's most dramatic transformations, a time when life emerges anew, and the groundwork for a thriving garden is laid. The techniques employed during this period can set the tone for the rest of the growing season, ensuring that plants are healthy, the soil is prepared, and all elements of the garden are harmonized with the energy of renewal. The key lies in understanding the subtle signals of spring and responding with care and precision.

The soil is the foundation of all life in the garden, and its transformation during spring is one of the first signs of the season's arrival. As the ground begins to thaw and dry, it becomes workable, signaling the gardener's opportunity to replenish and prepare it for planting. Careful observation is crucial; working the soil while it is still wet can lead to compaction, depriving roots of the air spaces they need to grow. A simple test—grabbing a handful of soil and squeezing it—reveals its readiness. If it crumbles easily rather than forming a sticky clump, the time has come to begin. Adding organic matter, such as well-aged compost or decomposed manure, enriches the soil with nutrients and enhances its structure, allowing plants to access the resources they need to thrive. A light turning with a fork or spade aerates the soil, bringing oxygen to the microorganisms that will work tirelessly to break down organic matter and feed the plants.

Clearing away the remnants of winter is another essential task. Fallen leaves, spent annuals, and other debris that accumulated during the colder months can harbor pests and diseases if left unchecked. However, this process should be approached with balance and care. Some debris may serve as shelter for overwintering beneficial insects, such as ladybugs or lacewing larvae. Removing it gradually and with attention to the life it supports helps maintain the ecosystem's health while tidying the space. Any plant material that shows signs of disease should be carefully disposed of, as pathogens can persist and spread if added to compost.

Spring is the time to evaluate perennials and decide on any necessary pruning or dividing. Many perennials benefit from division every few years, which not only rejuvenates the plants but also provides new growth to expand or share with others. Clumps that have grown too dense can be carefully dug up and separated, ensuring each division has a healthy portion of roots and shoots. This process invigorates the plants, allowing them to grow with renewed vigor. For shrubs and trees, pruning focuses on removing dead or damaged branches, which can inhibit healthy growth or create entry points for pests and diseases. The goal is to shape the plant while respecting its natural form, creating an open structure that allows light and air to penetrate.

The arrival of spring also signals the time to sow seeds and plant early crops, but timing is critical. Cool-season vegetables, such as lettuce, spinach, and peas, thrive in the gentle warmth of spring but struggle in the heat of summer. These should be planted as soon as the soil is workable, allowing them to establish themselves before temperatures climb. Starting seeds indoors can provide a head start for plants that require a longer growing season, such as tomatoes or peppers. Once the danger of frost has passed, these young plants can be transplanted into the garden, where they will continue to grow and produce through the warmer months.

Spring awakening techniques also involve creating conditions that encourage pollinators and other beneficial organisms to return to the garden. Early-blooming flowers, such as crocuses, daffodils, and hellebores, provide vital nectar and pollen for bees and other insects emerging from hibernation. These plants serve as a bridge, supporting pollinators until the broader array of summer blooms arrives. Providing water sources, such as shallow dishes filled with pebbles and water, further supports these creatures, ensuring they can stay hydrated as they work to pollinate the garden.

Mulching is another powerful spring technique, serving multiple purposes in the garden. A fresh layer of mulch, applied after the soil has warmed, helps retain moisture, suppress weeds, and regulate soil temperature. Organic mulches, such as straw, shredded bark, or pine needles, gradually break down over time, enriching the soil and feeding the microorganisms that sustain plant life. The timing of mulching is important; applying it too early, before the soil has warmed sufficiently, can trap cold air and delay plant growth.

Weed control is an inevitable part of spring gardening, as the warming soil awakens not only desired plants but also unwanted ones. Addressing weeds early, before they have a chance to establish deep roots or set seed, minimizes their impact throughout the growing season. Hand-pulling is effective for small infestations, while hoeing or cultivating can manage larger areas. Covering bare soil with mulch or ground covers prevents weed seeds from germinating, reducing the need for intervention later.

Spring is also the perfect time to assess and repair garden infrastructure. Paths, fences, trellises, and raised beds may have weathered damage during the winter and require attention. Replacing broken supports, tightening loose connections, and refreshing protective finishes ensures that these elements are ready to support the garden's growth. This maintenance prevents small issues from becoming larger problems later in the season.

One of the most rewarding aspects of spring awakening is the opportunity to connect with the garden on a deeper level. As plants unfurl their tender new leaves and the air fills with the hum of returning life, the rhythm of nature is palpable. Each task, whether sowing seeds or pruning branches, becomes an act of collaboration with the earth's cycles. The garden's awakening is not just a physical transformation but a renewal of the gardener's partnership with the land. By embracing the techniques that align with this moment of rebirth, gardeners lay the foundation for a season of abundance, beauty, and growth.

Summer Growth Management

The height of summer brings with it a burst of life and energy in the garden. Plants reach their full stride, leaves thicken and glisten in the sunlight, flowers bloom in dazzling arrays, and crops swell with promise. Yet, with this abundance comes the need for vigilant care and thoughtful management. Summer is a time of rapid growth and intense activity, but it also carries challenges: scorching heat, increased water demands, pest invasions, and competition among plants. To ensure the garden thrives during this season, it's essential to balance nurturing growth with managing its intensity.

One of the most pressing tasks during summer is managing water. As temperatures climb, plants lose moisture through transpiration, and the soil dries more quickly, making consistent watering critical. However, the method and timing of watering can make all the difference. Early mornings or late evenings are the optimal times to water, as cooler temperatures reduce evaporation and give plants a chance to absorb moisture before the heat sets in. Deep watering, where the soil is soaked to encourage deeper root systems, is far more beneficial than frequent, shallow watering that keeps roots near the surface and prone to drying out. Mulching around plants not only keeps the soil cool but also locks in moisture, reducing the frequency of watering while suppressing weeds that compete for resources. Rain barrels or other water collection systems can provide a supplemental source during dry spells, easing the burden on municipal supplies and adding a sustainable touch to garden care.

Pruning and deadheading are vital techniques for controlling the vigor of summer growth while encouraging continued productivity. For flowering plants, removing spent blooms, or deadheading, prevents energy from being diverted into seed production and instead redirects it toward creating new flowers. This simple act can extend bloom periods, keeping the garden colorful and vibrant well into late summer. For fruiting plants, removing damaged or overcrowded branches ensures that sunlight and airflow reach all parts of the plant, reducing the risk of fungal diseases and promoting even ripening. With shrubs and trees, summer pruning helps to maintain shape and remove suckers or water sprouts that sap energy from the main structure. While the temptation might be to let growth run wild in summer's abundance, careful pruning ensures that energy is channeled effectively, resulting in healthier, more productive plants.

Weed control is another task that cannot be overlooked during the summer months. Warm weather and ample sunlight create ideal conditions for weeds to thrive, often overtaking slower-growing plants if left unchecked. Hand-pulling weeds after a rain, when the soil is soft, ensures that roots are removed entirely, preventing regrowth. For larger areas, cultivating the soil with a hoe disrupts young weeds before they can establish themselves. Maintaining a layer of mulch around plants creates an additional barrier, smothering weed seeds and limiting their ability to germinate. Staying diligent about weed control not only keeps the garden tidy but also prevents competition for water, nutrients, and sunlight.

Pest management becomes a critical focus during summer, as the thriving garden attracts an array of visitors. While some insects, such as bees and butterflies, play essential roles as pollinators, others pose threats to plants. Aphids, caterpillars, and beetles can quickly damage foliage, stems, and fruits if left unchecked. Encouraging natural predators like ladybugs, lacewings, or birds is an effective way to keep pest populations under control. Companion planting—such as marigolds near tomatoes or nasturtiums with cucumbers—can deter certain pests through natural chemical signals. For more persistent problems, manual removal or targeted organic treatments, such as neem oil or insecticidal soap, can address infestations without harming beneficial insects. Monitoring the garden closely and acting promptly at the first sign of trouble prevents minor issues from escalating into significant challenges.

Supporting plants physically is another aspect of effective growth management during summer. As plants grow taller and heavier, their stems and branches may struggle to support the weight of flowers, fruits, or dense foliage. Staking, caging, or trellising provides the necessary support, preventing plants from collapsing under their own weight or being damaged by wind or rain. Tomatoes, peas, beans, and even some flowers like dahlias benefit greatly from being tied to sturdy supports, allowing them to grow upright and maintain better airflow. Proper support not only protects the plants but also makes harvesting and maintenance easier, reducing the risk of trampled stems or inaccessible fruits.

The intense summer heat can also strain plants, particularly those not adapted to high temperatures. Providing shade during the hottest parts of the day, whether through shade cloth, temporary structures, or strategically placed taller plants, can protect delicate crops and flowers. Lettuce, spinach, and other cool-season vegetables are especially prone to bolting in hot weather unless shielded from direct sunlight. Even heat-tolerant plants benefit from some respite, as prolonged exposure to extreme heat can cause stress, leading to reduced flowering or fruiting. Adjusting planting strategies to include heat-resistant varieties or intercropping with taller species to create natural shade can help the garden adapt to the challenges of summer.

Fertilization during this season plays a delicate role, as plants are actively growing and producing. Replenishing nutrients ensures continued vigor but must be done carefully to avoid over-fertilization, which can lead to excessive leaf growth at the expense of flowers and fruits. Compost tea, diluted fish emulsion, or balanced organic fertilizers provide a gentle boost, allowing plants to absorb what they need without overwhelming the soil. Timing is crucial, as applying fertilizers in the morning or evening when temperatures are cooler reduces the risk of burning plants. Regular but moderate feeding keeps plants sustained through their most productive period.

Finally, summer is a time to consider succession planting, a technique that keeps the garden continuously productive. As early crops like peas or radishes are harvested, their spaces can be replanted with fast-growing vegetables like beans or lettuce, ensuring that no area of the garden remains idle. Planning for staggered planting and harvesting creates a rhythm of continuous growth, making full use of the growing season while reducing the need for large-scale replanting later.

The summer garden, with all its energy and abundance, is a testament to the vitality of nature. Managing this growth effectively requires a combination of observation, timely action, and an understanding of the garden's needs. By balancing care with control, gardeners can navigate the challenges of heat and rapid development, transforming the season into one of beauty, productivity, and reward. The harmony achieved during these months becomes the foundation for the garden's continued success, echoing the rhythms of nature and the diligence of human hands.

Autumn Preparation Strategies

As the vibrant greens of summer give way to the rich golds, reds, and browns of autumn, the garden enters a period of transition. This season is not merely an ending but also a beginning, as the work done now will determine the garden's readiness for winter and its potential for renewal in spring. Autumn preparation is about nurturing the soil, protecting plants, and planning for the cycles to come. It's a time to reflect, tend, and lay the groundwork for future growth, ensuring that the garden rests well and awakens strong.

One of the first steps in autumn preparation is the careful clearing of annual plants that have completed their lifecycle. Vegetables like tomatoes, peppers, and squash, as well as summer flowers, begin to wither as the days shorten and temperatures drop. Removing these plants prevents the buildup of pests and diseases that could overwinter in the garden. However, not everything needs to be stripped away. Leaving healthy plant material, such as roots or stems, in the ground can contribute organic matter as it decomposes, enriching the soil. For gardeners seeking a more naturalistic approach, allowing certain seed heads to remain, such as those of sunflowers or coneflowers, provides food for birds and adds visual interest to the autumn landscape.

The soil itself demands particular attention during this time. After a season of growth and harvest, it may be depleted of nutrients and structure. Adding organic matter, such as compost, leaf mold, or well-rotted manure, restores its vitality and prepares it for the next growing season. Spreading these amendments in autumn allows them to break down over the winter months, integrating into the soil and becoming readily available to plants by spring. Cover crops, or green manures, offer another strategy for rejuvenating the soil. Sowing plants like clover, vetch, or rye helps prevent erosion, suppress weeds, and fix nutrients such as nitrogen into the soil. As these crops are tilled under in early spring, they enrich the soil with organic matter, creating a fertile foundation for new growth.

Perennial plants require a different kind of care as they prepare for dormancy. Dividing and transplanting perennials in autumn is ideal, as the cooler temperatures and increased rainfall reduce stress on the plants while encouraging root establishment. Overgrown clumps can be lifted, split, and replanted, ensuring that each division has enough roots and shoots to thrive. This not only revitalizes the plants but also provides an opportunity to expand the garden or share with others. For shrubs and trees, pruning dead or diseased branches promotes health and prevents damage during winter storms. Care should be taken not to prune too late in the season, as new growth stimulated by pruning may not harden off before frost, leaving it vulnerable.

Mulching is an essential autumn task, serving multiple purposes in the garden. A thick layer of organic mulch, such as straw, wood chips, or shredded leaves, insulates the soil, moderating temperature fluctuations and protecting plant roots from freezing. Mulch also reduces water loss, suppresses weeds, and breaks down over time to improve soil quality. Around perennials, shrubs, and trees, it creates a barrier that shields the crown and base from harsh winter conditions. Care must be taken not to pile mulch directly against plant stems, as this can trap moisture and encourage rot.

Autumn is also the time to plant spring-flowering bulbs like tulips, daffodils, and crocuses. These bulbs require a period of cold dormancy to bloom, making autumn planting crucial. Selecting a sunny spot with well-drained soil ensures their success. Planting them at the appropriate depth, typically two to three times the height of the bulb, protects them from freezing temperatures and hungry wildlife. For a natural look, scattering bulbs and planting them where they fall creates a more organic arrangement that mimics the patterns found in nature.

As the growing season winds down, it's important to assess and tidy garden infrastructure. Raised beds, trellises, and fences may have suffered wear and tear during the summer and need repair or reinforcement before winter. Tools and equipment should be cleaned, sharpened, and stored properly to prevent rust and damage. This maintenance ensures that everything will be ready when the garden awakens in spring, saving time and effort later.

Wildlife, too, benefits from thoughtful autumn preparation. Many creatures rely on gardens for shelter and sustenance during the colder months. Leaving patches of ground undisturbed provides habitat for overwintering insects, while brush piles, log stacks, or stone crevices offer sanctuary for small mammals, amphibians, and reptiles. Bird feeders stocked with seeds and suet help sustain feathered visitors when natural food sources dwindle. Creating a garden that supports wildlife through the winter weaves it into the broader ecosystem, enriching the garden's vitality and diversity.

Finally, autumn is a time for reflection and planning. Observing which plants thrived and which struggled provides valuable insights for the next growing season. Sketching out plans for crop rotation, new plantings, or design changes can transform the lessons of the past year into actionable strategies. It's also an ideal moment to collect seeds from heirloom vegetables or favorite flowers, preserving their genetics and ensuring a personal connection to the garden's legacy.

The rhythm of the seasons is evident in the tasks of autumn preparation. Each step, from clearing and enriching the soil to protecting and planning, aligns with the cycles of growth, dormancy, and renewal. By tending to the garden with care and foresight, gardeners create a space that not only endures the challenges of winter but also emerges in spring with renewed strength and promise. The work done in these crisp, cool days is an investment in the garden's future, a quiet act of stewardship that ensures its vitality for seasons to come.

Winter Rest and Planning

The quiet hush of winter descends upon the garden, blanketing it in frost and stillness. What appears to be a dormant landscape is, in truth, a time of subtle activity beneath the surface. Roots rest, soil organisms slow their pace, and the garden gathers strength for the seasons ahead. For the gardener, winter offers the opportunity to step back, observe, and plan with intention. It is a season of rest but also one of preparation, where careful thought and deliberate action lay the foundation for future growth.

Winter's stillness is deceptive; beneath the frost-covered soil, life persists. Perennials and bulbs remain nestled in their underground havens, their energy conserved for the burst of growth to come. The soil itself continues its quiet work, as microorganisms break down organic matter and enrich the earth. Recognizing this hidden activity reminds us of the importance of protecting the soil during the colder months. A blanket of mulch, straw, or even a thin layer of fallen leaves provides insulation, shielding the soil from temperature extremes and erosion. This protective layer also nurtures beneficial organisms, creating a stable environment for them to thrive. By preserving the integrity of the soil, the gardener ensures that it will be ready to support life when the thaw comes.

Winter is also a time to care for the structures and tools that make gardening possible. The physical demands of the growing season often leave fences, trellises, and raised beds in need of attention. Repairing and reinforcing these elements now, while the garden rests, avoids the scramble of maintenance during busier months. Tools, too, benefit from winter care. Cleaning and sharpening blades, oiling hinges, and storing them in a dry, protected place extend their lifespan and ensure they are ready for action when needed. This simple but essential upkeep reflects the idea that rest is not just about inactivity—it is about preparation for what lies ahead.

The starkness of winter offers a new perspective on the garden. Without the distraction of lush foliage and colorful blooms, the bones of the garden—its paths, structures, and overall layout—become more apparent. This clarity makes it an ideal time to evaluate the design, identifying areas that could be improved or reimagined. Perhaps a pathway needs widening, a bed could be reshaped, or a new focal point introduced. Sketching out these ideas, either on paper or through digital tools, transforms observations into actionable plans. The absence of immediate planting tasks allows for creativity to flow, unhurried and thoughtful.

Planning for the coming seasons extends beyond the garden's layout. Winter is the perfect time to reflect on the successes and challenges of the previous year. Which plants flourished, and which struggled to thrive? Did pests or diseases present recurring issues? Were there gaps in the harvest or flowering times? Answering these questions provides valuable insights that guide future decisions. Crop rotation, for example, becomes easier to plan when reflecting on what was planted and where. This practice not only prevents soil depletion but also disrupts the life cycles of pests and diseases. Similarly, selecting disease-resistant varieties or native plants suited to the local climate can address specific challenges identified during the previous season.

Seed catalogs, arriving in the mail or online during the heart of winter, are more than just a source of inspiration—they are tools for planning. Browsing through their pages, gardeners can explore new varieties, experiment with unfamiliar crops, or revisit trusted favorites. Creating a seed order list, organized by planting time and garden space, transforms the anticipation of spring into a concrete plan. Starting seeds indoors, particularly for plants with long growing seasons, becomes part of the winter rhythm. Carefully timed, this process ensures that young plants are ready to move outdoors as soon as conditions are favorable.

For those who grow edible crops, winter offers an opportunity to deepen the connection between garden and kitchen. Preserving the harvest through drying, freezing, or canning extends the garden's bounty into the colder months, providing a tangible reminder of its gifts. Planning meals around these preserved ingredients reinforces the idea that the garden is a year-round source of nourishment. It also inspires thoughts of what to grow in the coming year, based on what was most enjoyed or used frequently.

Wildlife, often overlooked in the dormant garden, plays an essential role even in winter. Birds, for instance, rely on feeders stocked with seeds and suet, as natural food sources become scarce. Providing water, through heated birdbaths or regularly refreshed dishes, ensures they stay hydrated despite freezing temperatures. These small acts of stewardship not only support wildlife but also bring life and movement to the quiet winter garden. Observing these creatures as they navigate the cold inspires a deeper appreciation for the interconnectedness of all things.

Winter is also a season for learning. With the garden at rest, there is time to read, attend workshops, or connect with other gardeners. Books and articles on soil health, companion planting, or sustainable practices deepen knowledge and spark new ideas. Joining local gardening groups or forums fosters a sense of community, where experiences are shared, and advice is exchanged. This period of intellectual growth enriches the gardener's understanding and prepares them to approach the coming seasons with renewed enthusiasm.

Though the garden sleeps, its influence endures, reminding us that rest is an essential part of any cycle. Winter is not a pause but a quieter rhythm, one that invites reflection, care, and planning. By embracing this season fully—tending to the soil, preparing tools, envisioning changes, and fostering connections—the gardener aligns with nature's ebb and flow. The effort made now, though less visible, is no less vital. It is a promise to the garden and to oneself, ensuring that when the first signs of spring appear, there is readiness to greet them with open hands and a clear vision. The garden's rest becomes the gardener's renewal, a partnership that continues to grow stronger with each passing season.

Transition Periods The In Between Times

The transition periods in a garden's lifecycle—those in-between times when one season yields to the next—are moments of flux, rich with opportunity and challenge. These intervals, often overlooked in their subtlety, are where the gardener's skill and intuition are most tested. Between the bold declarations of spring and summer or the quiet transformations of autumn and winter, lies a time of adjustment, a delicate balancing act where the remnants of one season mingle with the stirrings of the next. Understanding these transitions and responding to their nuances can elevate a garden's health and continuity, ensuring a seamless flow from one phase to another.

The shift from winter to spring begins as a whisper rather than a shout. Frost still clings to the mornings, and the soil may be too cold or wet for planting, but hints of renewal are everywhere. Buds begin to swell, and the earliest flowers—crocuses, snowdrops, and hellebores—push through the remnants of snow. The gardener must tread lightly in these moments, resisting the urge to act too quickly. Overeager efforts, such as working the soil before it has dried sufficiently, can cause compaction, making it harder for roots to penetrate later. Patience, paired with observation, is key. Preparing tools, organizing seeds, and planning layouts fill the gap while nature slowly awakens. As the soil warms and the days lengthen, the timing of early planting becomes critical. Cool-season crops like peas, lettuces, and radishes thrive in this transitional period, taking advantage of the mild temperatures before the heat of summer arrives. These early plantings bridge the gap between dormancy and full growth, initiating the garden's rhythm for the year ahead.

The transition from spring to summer is a time of rapid acceleration. Growth explodes across the garden, and the once-tender shoots of spring mature into robust plants. This period demands heightened attention, as the balance of water, nutrients, and light becomes paramount. Temperatures rise, and with them, the risk of stress to young plants. Mulching at this stage helps retain soil moisture and regulate temperature, providing a buffer against the intensifying sun. Succession planting plays a vital role during this time, ensuring that as one crop finishes, another takes its place. For example, after harvesting spring greens, the same space can be utilized for heat-loving crops like beans or peppers. This overlap keeps the garden productive and efficient, making use of every available inch of soil. The vigilance required during this transition extends to pest management as well. The warmth of early summer brings an influx of insects, both beneficial and harmful. Encouraging natural predators while addressing infestations quickly ensures that the garden remains balanced.

As summer begins to wane, the transition to autumn brings its own complexities. The intense heat subsides, and the garden's energy shifts from vigorous growth to ripening and consolidation. This period is a race against time for many crops, as the shortening days and cooling nights signal the end of their cycle. For the gardener, this is a moment to focus on harvesting and preserving the fruits of the season. Tomatoes, cucumbers, and squashes must be gathered before the first frost, while root crops like carrots and beets can often remain in the ground a bit longer, insulated by the cooling soil. Clearing spent plants and preparing the beds for fall crops becomes a priority. Late-season vegetables such as kale, spinach, and turnips thrive in the cooler temperatures and provide a second wave of productivity. These plantings, timed carefully, extend the garden's bounty well into autumn, bridging the gap as summer's abundance fades.

The transition from autumn to winter is perhaps the most contemplative of all. The garden slows visibly, its colors fading to muted tones, its textures softening under the weight of frost. This is a time of closure, but also of preparation. Perennials are cut back or left standing, depending on their role in the garden's ecosystem. Seed heads may be left to feed wildlife, while tender plants are mulched heavily or moved indoors to protect them from freezing temperatures. Composting takes center stage as the last of the garden's organic material—fallen leaves, spent plants, and kitchen scraps—is collected and processed. This compost, rich with the remnants of the season, will feed the soil in the spring, completing the cycle of renewal.

The in-between times are not solely about tasks and to-do lists; they are also about observation and learning. These transitions reveal the garden's rhythms and its responses to change. Watching how the soil behaves as it warms, how plants react to shifting light, or how wildlife adapts to the changing environment provides invaluable insights. These observations inform future decisions, allowing the gardener to anticipate challenges and seize opportunities. For instance, noting which areas of the garden dry out first in spring or which plants thrive in the cooler days of autumn can guide planting strategies and improve efficiency.

The transitions are also a reminder of the partnership between the gardener and nature. They demand flexibility and humility, an acknowledgment that the garden operates on its own timeline, not ours. Weather patterns may shift unexpectedly, delaying plantings or accelerating harvests. Pests may appear earlier or later than anticipated. By staying attuned to these changes and responding with adaptability, the gardener works in harmony with the natural world rather than against it.

In these in-between times, the garden teaches patience and resilience. It shows that growth is not always linear and that the pauses and shifts are as vital as the periods of full bloom. The transitions are where the garden's story unfolds, chapter by chapter, each one building upon the last. For the gardener, they are moments to engage deeply, to listen and learn, ensuring that the next season begins not with haste but with intention and care. These periods, though fleeting, hold the essence of what it means to tend a garden: to nurture, to adapt, and to grow alongside the ever-changing cycles of life.

Chapter 4: Water Management in Harmony

Natural Water Cycles

Water is the lifeblood of every ecosystem, cycling endlessly through the environment in a process that sustains all living things. In the garden, understanding and working with natural water cycles is fundamental to fostering a thriving, resilient space. Rainfall, evaporation, infiltration, and transpiration—each aspect of the water cycle is interconnected, shaping the soil, nourishing plants, and influencing the broader ecological balance. By aligning gardening practices with these natural processes, it becomes possible to create a system that conserves water, supports biodiversity, and enhances the health of the land.

Rain is the most tangible component of the water cycle and often the primary source of moisture for gardens. When it falls, its journey is far from straightforward. Depending on the soil's structure, vegetation, and slope, rainwater may seep into the ground, run off the surface, or evaporate back into the atmosphere. Managing how rain interacts with a garden is key to maximizing its benefits while minimizing waste and damage. Soil that is rich in organic matter absorbs water more effectively, reducing runoff and erosion. This organic matter acts like a sponge, holding moisture while allowing excess to drain, ensuring plants have a steady supply without becoming waterlogged. Covering the soil with mulch further enhances this process, protecting it from the compacting force of heavy rain and reducing evaporation.

For areas where rain is sporadic or unpredictable, capturing and storing water becomes essential. Rain barrels positioned under downspouts collect runoff from roofs, providing a free and sustainable water source. This stored rainwater is ideal for irrigation, as it is free from the chemicals often found in tap water. In larger spaces, constructing swales—shallow trenches designed to channel and hold rainwater—can slow its movement across the land, allowing it to infiltrate the soil rather than escaping as runoff. These techniques not only conserve water but also reduce strain on municipal systems during heavy rains, preventing flooding and pollution from excess stormwater.

Beneath the surface, water infiltrates the soil, replenishing groundwater reserves and making its way to plant roots. The speed and depth of infiltration depend on the soil's texture and composition. Sandy soils, with their large particles, drain quickly but struggle to retain moisture, while clay soils hold water tightly, making it less accessible to plants. Loamy soils, rich in organic material, strike a balance between drainage and retention, creating an ideal environment for roots to access water. Aerating compacted soil improves infiltration by creating spaces for water to move through, while planting deep-rooted species, such as native grasses, encourages water to penetrate further into the ground, nourishing deeper soil layers and reducing surface evaporation.

Transpiration, the process by which plants release water vapor through their leaves, plays a vital role in the water cycle. It not only cools plants but also contributes to local humidity levels, creating a microclimate that benefits surrounding vegetation. This cycle of uptake and release is driven by the roots' ability to draw moisture from the soil. Ensuring that plants have consistent access to water during periods of active growth supports healthy transpiration, which in turn regulates temperature and nutrient transport within the plant. Grouping plants with similar water needs simplifies irrigation and prevents overwatering, which can lead to root rot and other issues.

Evaporation, the transformation of water from liquid to vapor, is an inevitable part of the water cycle but one that gardeners can influence. Exposed soil loses moisture quickly under the sun's heat, leaving plants vulnerable to drought. Covering the ground with organic mulch—such as straw, bark chips, or shredded leaves—creates a protective barrier that reduces evaporation and keeps the soil cool. In addition to conserving water, mulch suppresses weeds, which compete for moisture, and gradually breaks down to enrich the soil. Choosing the right time to water also helps minimize evaporation; early mornings or late evenings, when temperatures are lower, allow water to soak into the ground rather than evaporating in the heat of midday.

Natural water cycles are deeply connected to the broader landscape. Wetlands, streams, and ponds act as reservoirs, holding water and slowly releasing it to sustain surrounding ecosystems. In the garden, creating features that mimic these natural systems can enhance resilience and biodiversity. A small pond, for example, provides a habitat for frogs, dragonflies, and other wildlife while storing water that can be used during dry periods. Planting along contours or creating terraces on slopes reduces runoff and erosion, helping water remain where it is most needed. Native plants, adapted to local rainfall patterns, thrive with minimal intervention, reducing the need for supplemental irrigation.

Climate change and increasing urbanization are placing unprecedented pressure on natural water cycles, making it more important than ever to adopt sustainable practices. Impervious surfaces, such as concrete and asphalt, prevent water from infiltrating the ground, leading to increased runoff and reduced groundwater recharge. In contrast, permeable pathways and planting areas allow water to soak into the soil, replenishing aquifers and reducing the risk of flooding. By designing gardens that prioritize infiltration and storage, it is possible to mitigate some of these challenges while creating beautiful and functional spaces.

The water cycle is not a static process but a dynamic and ever-changing system influenced by countless factors. By observing and respecting its patterns, gardeners can work in harmony with nature, using water wisely and efficiently. Simple practices, such as improving soil health, capturing rainwater, and planting wisely, have far-reaching effects, enhancing not only the garden itself but also the environment as a whole. These efforts remind us that water is not just a resource but a vital force, connecting all forms of life in an intricate web of interdependence. Through thoughtful stewardship, the garden becomes a microcosm of the broader natural world, reflecting the beauty and balance of water's perpetual journey.

Adaptive Irrigation Methods

Watering a garden or field is far more than simply pouring water over plants. It's a calculated effort to deliver the right amount of moisture to plants in a way that aligns with the natural environment and the gardener's specific needs. Adaptive irrigation methods are essential in today's world, where climate variability, water scarcity, and sustainability concerns demand innovative approaches. By tailoring irrigation practices to suit the soil, plant species, and local climate, it's possible to conserve water, reduce waste, and improve the health of the plants themselves. These methods bridge the gap between traditional techniques and modern technology, creating systems that are efficient, responsive, and environmentally conscious.

The heart of adaptive irrigation lies in understanding how water behaves within the soil. Different soil types retain and release moisture in unique ways, and irrigation strategies must account for these properties. Sandy soils, with their large particles, drain quickly and require frequent watering in smaller quantities to prevent leaching and ensure plants have consistent access to moisture. In contrast, clay soils hold water tightly, often leading to waterlogging if overwatered. For these soils, less frequent irrigation, applied slowly, allows water to penetrate deeply without overwhelming the surface. Loamy soils, often ideal for cultivation, balance drainage and retention, making them adaptable to a wider range of irrigation methods. Knowing the soil's texture and structure is the foundation of any effective irrigation approach.

Matching irrigation practices to a plant's needs is equally critical. Different species require varying amounts of water at different stages of growth. Seedlings, with their shallow and delicate root systems, need frequent, light watering to keep the upper layer of soil consistently moist. Established plants, on the other hand, benefit from deeper, less frequent watering that encourages roots to grow downward in search of moisture. This deeper rooting makes plants more resilient to drought and less reliant on surface water. High-water-demand crops, such as cucumbers or melons, require sustained irrigation throughout the growing season, while drought-tolerant varieties, like lavender or rosemary, thrive with minimal intervention once established. Grouping plants with similar water needs, known as hydrozoning, simplifies irrigation and ensures that no plant is over- or under-watered.

Timing plays a pivotal role in adaptive irrigation. The ideal time to water is early morning or late evening when temperatures are cooler and evaporation is minimized. Watering during the heat of the day leads to significant moisture loss as water evaporates before it can soak into the soil. Moreover, watering in the evenings reduces stress on plants but should be done carefully to avoid prolonged leaf wetness, which can encourage fungal diseases. The rhythm of irrigation must also adapt to seasonal changes. In spring, frequent rains might reduce the need for supplemental watering, while in summer, prolonged dry spells may necessitate a more active schedule.

Drip irrigation is one of the most efficient adaptive methods, delivering water directly to the plant's root zone through a network of tubes and emitters. This technique minimizes evaporation and runoff, as water is applied slowly and precisely where it is needed. Drip systems are particularly valuable in arid regions or for high-value crops where water conservation is paramount. They can be customized to fit any garden layout, from small beds to sprawling orchards, making them versatile and scalable. The slow, steady delivery of water also reduces weed growth, as areas between plants remain dry, depriving weeds of the moisture they need to germinate.

For larger-scale systems or areas with uneven terrain, sprinkler irrigation offers flexibility while still allowing for adjustments. Modern sprinklers can be programmed to target specific zones, ensuring even coverage without overwatering. Rotating or oscillating sprinklers mimic rainfall, distributing water across the landscape in a way that is gentle on plants and soil. However, care must be taken to avoid watering in windy conditions, which can lead to uneven distribution and waste. In regions where water is scarce, low-pressure sprinklers or micro-sprinklers can be used to deliver water with greater efficiency, focusing on the areas of highest need.

Rainwater harvesting is a time-tested practice that complements irrigation by providing an alternative water source. Collecting rainwater from roofs or other surfaces and storing it in tanks or barrels allows gardeners to reduce reliance on municipal or groundwater supplies. This stored rainwater, free of chemicals like chlorine, is often better suited for plants, particularly those sensitive to mineral buildup in tap water. Incorporating rainwater into irrigation systems not only conserves resources but also creates a buffer during periods of drought, ensuring a consistent supply even when rainfall is scarce.

Smart irrigation technology has emerged as a powerful tool for adapting watering practices to real-time conditions. Sensors placed in the soil measure moisture levels, sending data to a controller that adjusts irrigation schedules automatically. These systems ensure that water is applied only when necessary, preventing overwatering and conserving resources. Weather-based irrigation controllers take this a step further by integrating local climate data, such as rainfall forecasts and temperature trends, to fine-tune watering schedules. While the initial investment in smart technology can be significant, the long-term savings in water and labor make it an increasingly popular choice for both home gardeners and commercial growers.

Mulching works hand-in-hand with irrigation to make water use more efficient. By covering the soil with organic materials like straw, bark, or compost, moisture is trapped near the surface, reducing evaporation and keeping the soil cool. Mulch also suppresses weeds that compete with plants for water and nutrients, creating a harmonious environment for growth. Over time, as mulch breaks down, it adds organic matter to the soil, further improving its ability to retain moisture.

Adaptive irrigation methods are not just about technology or tools—they are about observation and flexibility. By paying close attention to the plants, soil, and weather, gardeners can respond to changes and fine-tune their approach. A sudden heatwave may require an increase in watering frequency, while an unexpected rainstorm calls for a pause to avoid oversaturating the soil. This dynamic relationship with water fosters a deeper understanding of the garden's needs and a more sustainable way of nurturing it.

Water is a finite and precious resource, and its careful management is essential for the health of both the garden and the planet. Adaptive irrigation, rooted in knowledge and guided by responsiveness, offers a path toward efficiency and sustainability. By embracing these methods, gardeners not only support their plants but also contribute to a broader culture of conservation, ensuring that future generations can continue to enjoy the life-giving benefits of water.

Chapter 5: Living Soil Ecosystem

Understanding Soil Life

Beneath the surface of every thriving garden lies a bustling world teeming with life. Soil, often regarded as simply dirt, is far more complex than it appears. It is a dynamic ecosystem in its own right, home to billions of organisms that work tirelessly to maintain its structure, fertility, and health. Understanding soil life is fundamental for any gardener or grower looking to cultivate a sustainable and productive environment. This hidden world, though invisible to the naked eye, is the foundation upon which all plant life depends, and nurturing it ensures the vitality of the entire garden.

Soil is alive with a diversity of organisms, from bacteria and fungi to earthworms and insects. The smallest of these, soil microbes, play an outsized role in its health. Bacteria, which are among the most abundant organisms in soil, specialize in breaking down organic matter into simpler compounds. This process releases essential nutrients, such as nitrogen, phosphorus, and potassium, making them available for plant uptake. Nitrogen-fixing bacteria, for instance, form symbiotic relationships with the roots of legumes, converting atmospheric nitrogen into a form plants can absorb. Without these microscopic workers, soil would quickly become depleted, unable to support the growth of healthy plants.

Fungi, another integral component of soil life, extend their threadlike networks, known as mycelium, through the soil. These networks act as conduits, transporting water and nutrients to plants in exchange for sugars produced through photosynthesis. Mycorrhizal fungi, in particular, form mutually beneficial relationships with plant roots, often increasing nutrient absorption by several orders of magnitude. This symbiosis is especially vital in nutrient-poor soils, where the fungi's ability to scavenge for resources far beyond the reach of roots gives plants a critical advantage. Fungi also play a role in breaking down tougher organic materials, such as lignin in woody debris, contributing to the formation of humus—a stable, nutrient-rich component of soil.

Larger soil organisms, such as earthworms, millipedes, and beetles, contribute to soil health in more visible ways. Earthworms, often called "nature's plow," aerate the soil as they burrow, creating channels that improve water infiltration and root penetration. Their digestive processes break down organic matter, producing nutrient-packed castings that enrich the soil. Millipedes and beetles, meanwhile, shred larger plant debris into smaller pieces, accelerating decomposition and making it easier for microbes and fungi to do their work. These creatures, though small in size, are vital engineers of the soil ecosystem, ensuring its structure remains porous and its nutrients are continuously recycled.

The interactions between these organisms create a web of activity that drives the soil's ability to support life. At the center of this web is organic matter, the fuel that powers soil life. Organic matter consists of decaying plant residues, animal remains, and microbial byproducts, all of which are broken down by soil organisms into their component parts. This process not only releases nutrients but also improves the soil's physical properties, increasing its ability to retain water and resist erosion. Over time, some of this organic material becomes humus, a stable substance that acts as a long-term reservoir of nutrients and carbon.

Soil structure, the arrangement of particles and pores, is both influenced by and essential to soil life. A well-structured soil contains aggregates—clusters of soil particles bound together by organic matter and microbial secretions. These aggregates create a network of pores that allow air, water, and roots to move freely through the soil. Compacted or degraded soils, by contrast, lack this structure, making it difficult for organisms to thrive and for plants to access the resources they need. Maintaining soil structure requires protecting it from excessive disturbance, such as over-tilling, which can break apart aggregates and disrupt the delicate balance of life within.

Soil pH, the measure of its acidity or alkalinity, also plays a crucial role in shaping soil life. Most soil organisms and plants prefer a slightly acidic to neutral pH, typically ranging from 6.0 to 7.5. Outside this range, the availability of key nutrients can diminish, and certain organisms may struggle to survive. For example, acidic soils often support fewer bacteria but may favor fungi, shifting the balance of microbial activity. Testing and, if necessary, amending the soil to maintain an optimal pH ensures that its microbial community remains diverse and active.

Water is another critical factor in the health of soil life. Too much water can create anaerobic conditions, where oxygen is scarce, leading to the dominance of organisms that thrive in such environments, some of which can produce toxins harmful to plants. Conversely, too little water can stress or kill soil organisms, halting the processes that sustain fertility. Striking a balance, through proper irrigation and drainage, supports the soil's inhabitants and maintains the conditions under which they excel.

One of the most effective ways to promote soil life is by minimizing practices that disrupt it. Reducing or eliminating synthetic chemical inputs, such as pesticides and herbicides, allows beneficial organisms to thrive without interference. Cover cropping, the practice of planting non-harvest crops like clover or rye, protects the soil from erosion, adds organic matter, and fosters a diverse microbial community. Similarly, composting returns valuable nutrients and organic material to the soil, feeding its inhabitants and enhancing its overall health.

Observing the soil closely provides valuable insights into its vitality. The presence of earthworms, the smell of rich organic matter, and the texture of the soil itself are all indicators of its condition. Healthy soil teems with activity, its life evident in the way it crumbles between your fingers, smells earthy and complex, and supports robust plant growth above ground. By paying attention to these signs and adjusting practices accordingly, gardeners and growers can build a resilient system that supports both plants and the broader ecosystem.

Soil life is a testament to nature's ingenuity, a hidden network that sustains the visible beauty of the garden. It reminds us that the health of what lies beneath directly influences what flourishes above. By nurturing this vibrant community, protecting its delicate balance, and working in harmony with its rhythms, we ensure not only the success of our plants but also the longevity of the soil itself—an inheritance for generations to come. Understanding and respecting soil life transforms gardening into an act of stewardship, one that connects us to the intricate web of life beneath our feet.

Natural Fertility Cycles

The fertility of the earth is not simply a matter of adding nutrients to soil; it is the result of complex, interconnected cycles that sustain life. Nature operates through a continuous process of renewal, where nutrients flow through living organisms, organic matter, and the soil itself in a harmonious balance. Understanding these natural fertility cycles is essential for anyone who seeks to nurture the land sustainably. By working with these cycles rather than disrupting them, it is possible to cultivate healthy, productive soil that supports robust plant growth while reducing dependence on synthetic inputs.

At the heart of natural fertility is the decomposition of organic matter. Leaves fall, plants die back, and animals leave behind waste—all of which become raw materials for the soil's ecosystem. Microorganisms, such as bacteria and fungi, break down this organic material into simpler compounds. As they work, they release nutrients like nitrogen, phosphorus, and potassium, which are essential for plant growth. This process, known as mineralization, transforms the stored energy of organic matter into forms that plants can absorb through their roots. Without this constant recycling of nutrients, even the richest soil would eventually become barren.

Nitrogen, often referred to as the engine of plant growth, is a key element in natural fertility cycles. Though it is abundant in the atmosphere, plants cannot use it in its gaseous form. Instead, nitrogen must be "fixed" into a usable form by specific types of bacteria. Some of these bacteria live freely in the soil, while others, such as those in the genus Rhizobium, form symbiotic relationships with the roots of legumes. These bacteria convert atmospheric nitrogen into ammonia, which is then further transformed into nitrates and nitrites—the forms plants can readily absorb. When plants die or shed leaves, the nitrogen they contain is returned to the soil, where it is processed again, continuing the cycle. This natural nitrogen economy is both efficient and sustainable, providing a renewable source of fertility that requires no external inputs.

Phosphorus and potassium, while less abundant than nitrogen, are equally vital. Phosphorus supports energy transfer within plants, playing a crucial role in photosynthesis and root development. Potassium regulates water uptake, disease resistance, and overall plant health. These nutrients are released into the soil as rocks weather over time and as organic matter decomposes. Unlike nitrogen, which cycles relatively quickly, phosphorus and potassium move more slowly through the ecosystem. Their availability can be influenced by soil pH and microbial activity, both of which affect how easily plants can access these nutrients. Encouraging the natural processes that release and recycle these elements ensures a steady supply without the need for chemical fertilizers.

The role of soil organisms in fertility cycles cannot be overstated. Earthworms, for example, consume organic matter and excrete nutrient-rich castings that improve soil structure and fertility. Mycorrhizal fungi form networks that extend far beyond plant roots, accessing nutrients in distant soil pockets and sharing them with their host plants in exchange for sugars. Even the smallest creatures, such as nematodes and protozoa, contribute by feeding on bacteria and fungi, releasing nutrients in forms that plants can absorb. This intricate web of interactions creates a self-sustaining system, where each organism plays a role in maintaining the balance of fertility.

Cover crops and green manures are tools that mimic and enhance these natural cycles. When planted during the off-season, cover crops like clover, vetch, or rye protect the soil from erosion and suppress weeds. More importantly, they add organic matter and nutrients when they are tilled into the soil or left to decompose in place. Leguminous cover crops, in particular, fix nitrogen through their association with root-dwelling bacteria, enriching the soil for subsequent plantings. These practices not only boost fertility but also improve soil structure and water retention, creating an environment where natural cycles can thrive.

Composting is another way to harness the power of natural fertility cycles. By collecting plant material, kitchen scraps, and other organic waste, gardeners can create a concentrated source of nutrients that mirrors the decomposition processes occurring in the wild. The heat generated by microbial activity within a compost pile accelerates the breakdown of organic matter, producing a rich, dark humus that can be returned to the soil. Compost not only adds nutrients but also enhances the soil's ability to retain moisture and resist erosion. It is a closed-loop system, turning waste into a valuable resource and reducing the need for external inputs.

Crop rotation is an ancient practice rooted in the principles of natural fertility. By alternating the types of plants grown in a given area, it disrupts the life cycles of pests and diseases while preventing the depletion of specific nutrients. For example, following a nitrogen-hungry crop like corn with a nitrogen-fixing legume replenishes the soil's reserves. This cyclical approach mimics the diversity found in natural ecosystems, where no single species dominates for long. The result is healthier soil, more resilient plants, and a reduced need for synthetic fertilizers.

The interaction between plants and the soil is not one-sided; plants actively contribute to fertility cycles through their roots. As they grow, roots exude sugars, amino acids, and other compounds that feed soil microbes. These exudates stimulate microbial activity, increasing the breakdown of organic matter and the release of nutrients. In return, the microbes support plant growth, creating a feedback loop that benefits both parties. Plants also play a role in stabilizing the soil, reducing erosion and helping to retain nutrients within the ecosystem.

Water is an integral part of fertility cycles, as it facilitates the movement of nutrients through the soil and into plant roots. However, excessive water can wash nutrients away, especially in soils with poor structure. Practices such as mulching and maintaining ground cover reduce runoff, keeping nutrients where they are needed and protecting the integrity of the soil. Managing water wisely ensures that fertility cycles remain intact and that the soil continues to support life.

Natural fertility cycles are resilient but not indestructible. Over-tilling, monoculture farming, and the excessive use of synthetic chemicals can disrupt these cycles, depleting the soil and harming the organisms that sustain it. Restoring and preserving these cycles requires a commitment to practices that align with nature's rhythms. By fostering biodiversity, adding organic matter, and minimizing disturbances, it is possible to create a system where fertility is continuously renewed.

The cycles that govern soil fertility are a testament to nature's ingenuity, a reminder that life sustains life through endless renewal. By understanding and respecting these processes, we can work with the land rather than against it, ensuring that its productivity endures for generations to come. The soil, alive with its unseen networks, offers everything plants need to thrive when its natural balance is protected. In embracing these cycles, we not only grow healthier plants but also deepen our connection to the earth itself.

Composting with the Seasons

Composting is a dynamic process, one that shifts and changes with the rhythm of the seasons. Each part of the year brings unique conditions that influence how organic material breaks down and how compost piles behave. Understanding these seasonal shifts and adapting to them allows gardeners to maximize the efficiency of composting while working in harmony with nature's cycles. Whether it's the brisk pace of decomposition in spring, the heat-fueled acceleration of summer, the steady preparation of autumn, or the slower, deliberate breakdown of winter, each season offers its own opportunities and challenges.

Spring is a season of renewal, and composting mirrors this resurgence of activity. As temperatures rise and the soil awakens, microbial life in compost piles becomes more active. The damp conditions left behind by winter snow or rain provide a favorable environment for bacteria and fungi to thrive. This is the ideal time to assess the state of your compost pile and give it a jumpstart. Turning the pile helps aerate it, introducing oxygen that supports aerobic decomposition and prevents the pile from becoming anaerobic, which can lead to unpleasant odors. Adding fresh green materials, such as grass clippings, vegetable scraps, and young weeds (before they set seed), provides the nitrogen necessary to balance the carbon-rich browns that may have accumulated over the winter, like dried leaves or straw. The balance between greens and browns, often called the carbon-to-nitrogen ratio, is critical at this time to create the perfect environment for decomposition. Spring is also an excellent opportunity to use partially finished compost in garden beds, as its nutrients can feed emerging plants while continuing to break down in the soil.

Summer brings a surge of heat, both in the environment and within the compost pile itself. The higher temperatures of the season accelerate microbial activity, often creating the conditions for the pile to reach its peak internal heat. This thermophilic stage is critical for breaking down tougher materials, such as woody stems or fibrous roots, as well as killing off weed seeds and pathogens. To maintain these temperatures, compost piles need to be managed carefully. Regular turning ensures even heating throughout the pile, while consistent moisture levels are essential to prevent the pile from drying out in the summer sun. Adding water during dry spells keeps the process moving, but care must be taken not to overwater, as excessive moisture can drown the aerobic microbes and slow decomposition. Summer gardens produce an abundance of green material, from spent plants to kitchen scraps, which can be added to the pile. However, it's important to mix these with browns to avoid creating a slimy, compacted mess. The rapid decomposition of summer often means that finished compost can be ready in as little as two to three months, providing a rich amendment for mid-season planting or soil improvement.

Autumn is a season of abundance for composters, as gardens and landscapes provide an almost endless supply of organic material. Leaves, often considered the gold standard of composting browns, fall in great quantities, offering a high-carbon resource that balances the nitrogen-heavy materials from summer. Shredding leaves before adding them to the pile speeds up their breakdown, while layering them with green material prevents them from matting and creating an impermeable barrier. Autumn is also a time to incorporate garden clean-up debris, such as spent vegetable plants, annual flowers, and small prunings. However, diseased plants or invasive weeds should be excluded to avoid introducing problems into the finished compost. As temperatures cool, the microbial activity in the pile begins to slow, but the addition of fresh materials and occasional turning can keep the process going well into the season. Covering the pile with a tarp or a layer of straw helps retain heat and moisture, extending the active composting period before winter sets in.

Winter slows everything down, including the composting process. Cold temperatures reduce microbial activity to a crawl, and in freezing conditions, decomposition may temporarily halt altogether. However, this doesn't mean composting has to stop. Organic material can still be added to the pile, where it will begin to break down as soon as temperatures rise again. To prevent the pile from becoming overly compacted or waterlogged by snow and ice, it's helpful to continue adding a mix of greens and browns, even if the decomposition is less active. Covering the pile with a tarp or insulating it with straw or cardboard can help maintain some warmth and protect it from excessive moisture. For those with smaller spaces, compost bins or tumblers can be particularly useful in winter, as they contain the material and make it easier to manage. By the time spring returns, the materials added during winter will already be partially decomposed, giving the pile a head start for the season.

Throughout the year, the act of composting offers a way to stay connected to the cycles of nature. It transforms what might otherwise be waste into a resource that enriches the soil, feeds plants, and supports the broader ecosystem. By observing the changes in the environment and adjusting composting practices accordingly, gardeners can align their efforts with the natural rhythms of the seasons. Each season brings its own lessons, from the energy of spring to the patience of winter, reminding us that the process of transformation is ongoing and ever-evolving.

Composting with the seasons is not just about managing a pile of organic matter; it's about participating in the continuous cycle of growth, decay, and renewal that sustains life. The compost pile becomes a microcosm of the natural world, a place where the energy of the sun, the activity of microbes, and the gardener's care come together to create something new. By embracing the seasonal shifts in composting, we not only enrich our gardens but also deepen our understanding of the interconnectedness of all living things. Through this practice, we contribute to a system that nourishes the earth while teaching us the value of patience, observation, and balance.

Soil Structure and Health

Healthy soil is the foundation of a thriving ecosystem, and its structure is what determines its ability to sustain plant life, support water movement, and house a diverse array of organisms. Soil structure refers to how individual particles—sand, silt, and clay—bind together to form aggregates. These aggregates create the spaces, or pores, that allow air and water to move through the soil. When the structure is intact and well-balanced, it fosters an environment where roots can grow deeply, nutrients can cycle effectively, and microorganisms can flourish. Understanding soil structure and its connection to overall soil health is essential for cultivating land that remains fertile and productive over time.

At the core of soil structure are aggregates, which are clusters of soil particles bound together by organic matter, microbial secretions, and physical forces. These aggregates vary in size, from microscopic clumps to larger, visible structures that give soil its texture and consistency. Well-aggregated soil is often described as "crumbly," resembling the texture of a sponge cake. This crumbly nature is a sign of good health, as it indicates the presence of stable pores that allow water, air, and roots to penetrate the soil. In contrast, poorly aggregated soil, often compacted or crusted, restricts these essential movements, leading to waterlogging, erosion, and poor plant growth.

Organic matter plays a critical role in forming and maintaining soil structure. It acts as a glue that binds particles together, creating stable aggregates. As plant residues, animal wastes, and decomposing organisms break down, they release compounds that enhance aggregation. Humus, the final product of decomposition, is particularly effective in improving structure. Not only does it bind particles, but it also increases the soil's water-holding capacity, making it more resilient to drought. In soils where organic matter is depleted, structure begins to break down, leading to compaction and a loss of fertility.

Water is both a friend and a foe to soil structure. While moisture is essential for the chemical and biological processes that sustain soil health, excessive water can disrupt aggregates, causing particles to separate and clog pores. This separation, known as dispersion, often occurs in soils with high clay content when they become saturated. On the other hand, in sandy soils, water drains too quickly, limiting the time available for plants to absorb nutrients. Maintaining an optimal balance of moisture is therefore crucial. Practices like mulching, incorporating organic matter, and planting cover crops help regulate soil moisture levels, preventing the extremes of saturation and drought that can harm structure.

Compaction is one of the most significant threats to soil structure and health. It occurs when soil particles are pressed together, reducing pore space and making it difficult for roots, water, and air to move freely. Heavy machinery, repeated foot traffic, and over-tilling are common causes of compaction. The effects are often visible in the form of hardpan layers, which are dense zones just below the surface where roots struggle to penetrate. Compacted soil not only restricts plant growth but also increases runoff, as water cannot infiltrate effectively. Preventing compaction involves minimizing disturbance, avoiding work on wet soils, and using techniques like aeration or planting deep-rooted species to break up compacted layers naturally.

Erosion further exacerbates the degradation of soil structure. When soil lacks vegetation or cover, wind and water carry away its top layer, which is often the most nutrient-rich and biologically active. Without this protective layer, the remaining soil becomes more vulnerable to compaction and crusting. Erosion not only depletes the land but also contributes to water pollution, as sediments carry nutrients and chemicals into waterways. Planting ground covers, maintaining mulch, and designing landscapes to slow water movement are effective strategies to combat erosion and preserve soil structure.

The biological activity within soil is closely linked to its structure, and the two form a feedback loop that determines overall health. Earthworms, for instance, are natural engineers of soil structure. As they burrow, they create channels that improve aeration and drainage. Their castings, rich in nutrients, further enhance aggregation. Microorganisms such as bacteria and fungi also play a vital role. Fungal hyphae weave through soil particles, binding them together, while bacteria produce sticky substances that cement aggregates. The diversity and abundance of these organisms are indicators of soil health, as they reflect a thriving ecosystem capable of supporting plant growth.

Soil pH, the measure of its acidity or alkalinity, influences both structure and health. In highly acidic or alkaline soils, the availability of essential nutrients can be limited, and microbial activity may decline. For example, in acidic soils, the binding agents that hold aggregates together can weaken, leading to structural instability. Testing soil pH and making adjustments, such as adding lime to raise pH or sulfur to lower it, helps maintain a balance that supports both structure and biological activity.

Tillage, while sometimes necessary, can have a profound impact on soil structure. Excessive or improper tilling breaks apart aggregates, disrupts microbial communities, and exposes organic matter to rapid decomposition, leading to a decline in fertility. Reduced-till or no-till practices, on the other hand, preserve structure by minimizing disturbance. These methods rely on natural processes, like root growth and microbial activity, to maintain aggregation and improve soil health over time. Cover cropping and crop rotation complement these practices by adding organic matter and reducing erosion, further protecting the structure.

The visual and tactile qualities of soil often provide clues about its structure and health. Soil that crumbles easily when handled, retains moisture without becoming waterlogged, and supports robust plant growth is typically in good condition. Conversely, soil that forms hard clods, feels overly sandy, or crusts on the surface may indicate structural issues. Observing how water behaves—whether it pools, infiltrates quickly, or runs off—also reveals important information about the state of the soil.

Maintaining soil structure and health requires a holistic approach that considers the physical, chemical, and biological aspects of the soil. It is not a static goal but an ongoing process of observation, adjustment, and care. By focusing on practices that build organic matter, prevent compaction, and enhance biological activity, it is possible to create a resilient soil system that supports life above and below the surface. Healthy soil structure is the bridge between the unseen world of microorganisms and the visible vitality of plants, a reminder that the most important work often happens beneath our feet. Through thoughtful stewardship, the soil becomes not just a medium for growth but a thriving ecosystem in its own right, capable of sustaining life for generations.

Microorganism Partners

The soil beneath our feet is alive with an astonishing array of microorganisms, each playing a unique role in sustaining the delicate balance of life. These unseen partners are the foundation of healthy soil, working tirelessly to break down organic matter, recycle nutrients, and foster the growth of plants. While they may be invisible to the naked eye, their presence is crucial, forming intricate networks and symbiotic relationships that drive the vitality of any ecosystem. Understanding these microorganisms and their contributions is key to unlocking the full potential of soil, ensuring that it thrives as a living, breathing entity.

Bacteria, among the smallest of soil organisms, are also some of the most essential. These single-celled powerhouses exist in staggering numbers, often numbering billions in just a single gram of soil. Their primary role is decomposition, breaking down organic matter into simpler compounds that plants can readily absorb as nutrients. Some bacteria specialize in nitrogen fixation, a process that transforms atmospheric nitrogen into forms like ammonium and nitrate, which plants depend on for growth. These nitrogen-fixing bacteria, often found in the root nodules of legumes, form partnerships with plants that are mutually beneficial. In exchange for the sugars produced through photosynthesis, the bacteria provide a steady supply of nitrogen, enriching the soil in the process. This natural mechanism reduces the need for synthetic fertilizers, making it a cornerstone of sustainable agriculture.

Fungi, another vital group of soil microorganisms, operate in ways that complement the work of bacteria. Unlike bacteria, which are primarily involved in breaking down simpler organic materials, fungi excel at decomposing tough, fibrous substances like lignin found in wood. This makes them indispensable in recycling plant debris and contributing to the formation of humus, a stable organic material that improves soil structure and water retention. Mycorrhizal fungi, in particular, are renowned for their symbiotic relationships with plant roots. These fungi extend their threadlike hyphae into the soil, forming vast networks that dramatically increase a plant's ability to access water and nutrients, especially phosphorus. In return, the fungi receive carbohydrates from the plant. This exchange not only boosts plant growth but also enhances the overall health of the soil, as the fungal networks stabilize aggregates and improve its structure.

Actinomycetes, a lesser-known but equally important group of microorganisms, occupy a middle ground between bacteria and fungi. These filamentous bacteria are responsible for breaking down more resistant organic materials, such as cellulose and chitin, which other microbes struggle to process. Their activity contributes to the earthy smell of healthy soil, a scent that signals microbial abundance and activity. Actinomycetes also produce antibiotics that suppress harmful pathogens, protecting plants from diseases and promoting a balanced microbial community. Their presence is a marker of robust soil health, as they thrive in environments rich in organic matter and well-aerated conditions.

Protozoa, microscopic single-celled organisms, play a more indirect but no less important role in soil ecosystems. By feeding on bacteria and other smaller microorganisms, protozoa help regulate microbial populations and release nitrogen into the soil in a form that plants can absorb. This grazing activity creates a ripple effect, stimulating bacterial growth and enhancing nutrient cycling. Protozoa thrive in moist soils with ample organic matter, and their presence indicates a dynamic and well-functioning microbial community.

Nematodes, often called roundworms, are another group of microorganism partners that contribute to soil health. While some nematodes are plant parasites, the majority are beneficial, preying on bacteria, fungi, and other soil organisms. This predation not only controls microbial populations but also releases nutrients locked within their prey, making them available to plants. Certain nematodes also help decompose organic matter, contributing to the overall nutrient cycle. The diversity of nematodes in soil is often used as an indicator of its biological health, as their abundance reflects a balanced ecosystem.

The interactions between these microorganisms create a web of activity that forms the backbone of soil fertility. Each group plays a distinct role, but their contributions are interconnected. For example, the waste products of one organism often become the food source for another, creating a continuous cycle of nutrient exchange. This interconnectedness ensures that nutrients are recycled efficiently, organic matter is broken down, and harmful pathogens are kept in check. The result is a soil ecosystem that supports plant growth while maintaining its own health and resilience. activities, however, can disrupt this delicate balance. Overuse of chemical fertilizers, pesticides, and intensive tillage can harm microbial communities, reducing their diversity and abundance. This not only weakens the soil's ability to sustain life but also makes it more vulnerable to erosion, compaction, and nutrient depletion. Restoring and protecting microbial life requires practices that prioritize soil health, such as adding organic matter, reducing chemical inputs, and minimizing disturbance. Composting, cover cropping, and crop rotation are particularly effective in fostering microbial diversity, creating an environment where these organisms can thrive.

Observing the effects of healthy microorganisms is often as simple as examining the plants they support. Vibrant growth, deep green foliage, and strong root systems are all signs of a well-functioning soil ecosystem. Conversely, stunted growth, yellowing leaves, and poor yields may indicate an imbalance in the microbial community. Soil testing can provide more specific insights, revealing the levels of organic matter, pH, and microbial activity that influence plant health.

The partnerships between microorganisms and soil are a testament to the intricacy and efficiency of natural systems. These tiny organisms, unseen yet indispensable, are the engines that drive the cycles of life, transforming organic matter into the nutrients that sustain plants, animals, and humans alike. By understanding and nurturing these partnerships, we not only improve the productivity of the land but also contribute to the broader goal of sustainability. Healthy soil teeming with microbial life is a legacy that benefits not only the present but also future generations, ensuring that the earth remains fertile and full of potential.

Chapter 6: Plant Communities and Succession

Natural Plant Groupings

Nature has an intrinsic way of arranging itself into harmonious patterns, and this is particularly evident in the way plants grow together in ecosystems. Natural plant groupings, also known as plant communities, are not random collections of species but carefully balanced assemblies shaped by climate, soil, water availability, and interactions among organisms. These groupings are not only aesthetically pleasing but also resilient, efficient, and sustainable. By mimicking these natural arrangements, gardeners, farmers, and land managers can design landscapes that thrive with minimal intervention, promoting biodiversity while conserving resources.

In any untouched environment—be it a meadow, forest, or wetland—the plants growing there have adapted to the specific conditions of that area over time. Each species occupies a niche, fulfilling a role that contributes to the overall health of the system. Grasses may dominate open spaces, their dense root systems holding the soil together and preventing erosion. Shrubs and understory plants fill the middle layer, thriving in partial shade and providing food or shelter for wildlife. Towering trees form a protective canopy, influencing the microclimate beneath them by regulating temperature and humidity. Together, these layers create a self-sustaining network, with each plant contributing to the stability and functionality of the whole.

One of the defining features of natural plant groupings is their ability to share resources rather than compete destructively. Plants with complementary needs often grow together, each drawing from a different part of the soil or performing a unique role within the ecosystem. For example, in a temperate forest, deep-rooted trees access water and nutrients from lower soil layers, while shallow-rooted plants utilize the upper layers. Similarly, nitrogen-fixing plants like clover or lupine enrich the soil, benefiting neighboring species that rely on higher nitrogen levels. These symbiotic relationships allow the group to thrive collectively, even under challenging conditions.

Biodiversity is another hallmark of natural plant groupings. A diverse community, with a mix of species, is more resilient to pests, diseases, and environmental stresses. In contrast, monocultures—where only one species is cultivated—are vulnerable because a single threat can devastate the entire population. In natural ecosystems, the variety of plants supports a wide range of insects, birds, and other animals, creating a balanced web of life. Pollinators, for instance, are drawn to flowering species, while predatory insects feed on pests, reducing the need for human intervention. This interconnectedness is a reminder that plant groupings do not exist in isolation but are part of a larger, living system.

In arid regions, for example, native plant groupings have evolved to make the most of scarce water resources. Succulents, cacti, and drought-tolerant grasses grow together, their adaptations allowing them to survive extreme conditions. Some plants have waxy coatings to reduce water loss, while others store moisture in their tissues. Their roots often spread wide but remain shallow, capturing rainfall before it evaporates. In these environments, ground covers such as low-growing shrubs reduce evaporation by shading the soil, while taller plants act as windbreaks, protecting smaller species from desiccating winds. This kind of cooperation within a plant community ensures that even in the harshest climates, life can persist.

Woodlands and forests, on the other hand, demonstrate a vertical complexity that maximizes the use of available light, water, and nutrients. In these environments, plants are arranged in layers, with towering trees forming the canopy and smaller species occupying the understory. Ground-level plants thrive in the filtered light that penetrates the canopy, creating a lush, multi-tiered ecosystem. Trees like oaks or maples dominate the upper layers, while shrubs such as azaleas fill in the middle. At ground level, ferns, mosses, and wildflowers cover the soil, preventing erosion while adding beauty and biodiversity. The leaf litter and decomposing organic matter from these plants feed the soil, completing the nutrient cycle and fostering the next generation of growth.

Grasslands and prairies, though less vertically diverse, are equally fascinating in their arrangement. These open landscapes are often dominated by perennial grasses, interspersed with wildflowers and legumes. Grasses, with their fibrous roots, excel at stabilizing the soil and capturing rainfall, while wildflowers attract pollinators and add bursts of color to the scene. Legumes play a critical role by fixing nitrogen in the soil, improving fertility for the entire community. Together, these plants create a dense, interwoven network that prevents erosion, supports wildlife, and thrives in conditions that might seem inhospitable to less-adapted species.

Wetlands provide yet another example of natural plant groupings, showing how plants can adapt to waterlogged soils and fluctuating water levels. In these environments, reeds and sedges dominate, their spongy tissues designed to tolerate water saturation. Aquatic plants like water lilies float on the surface, capturing sunlight and providing habitat for insects and fish. Shrubs and trees such as willows or alders grow along the edges, stabilizing the banks and filtering runoff. These ecosystems are not only vital for biodiversity but also act as natural water purifiers, removing pollutants and improving water quality.

For those cultivating land or designing gardens, observing and emulating natural plant groupings offers a wealth of benefits. By choosing species that naturally coexist, it is possible to create landscapes that require fewer inputs, such as water, fertilizers, or pesticides. Companion planting, a practice rooted in the principles of natural groupings, pairs plants that benefit one another. For instance, growing marigolds near vegetables can deter pests, while planting sunflowers alongside beans provides support for climbing vines. These strategies reduce the need for synthetic chemicals and create a more sustainable, self-sufficient ecosystem.

Natural groupings also teach the importance of planting for the local climate and soil conditions. Native plants, which have evolved in a particular region, are best suited to its challenges and often require less maintenance than non-native species. They are also more likely to support local wildlife, preserving the ecological balance. By working with nature rather than against it, gardeners can create spaces that are both beautiful and functional, fostering biodiversity while reducing environmental impact.

The wisdom of natural plant groupings lies in their adaptability, efficiency, and interconnectedness. These communities demonstrate that diversity and cooperation are the keys to resilience, offering a model for sustainable land management. By understanding and applying these principles, it becomes possible to cultivate landscapes that are not only productive but also harmonious with the natural world. The lessons drawn from these groupings remind us that the most sustainable systems are those that mirror the intricate balance found in nature itself.

Companion Planting Strategies

Plants, much like people, often thrive when they have the right companions nearby. In the natural world, certain plants grow together in ways that benefit one another, forming partnerships that enhance growth, protect against pests, and even improve soil health. Companion planting draws on these natural relationships, offering a thoughtful approach to cultivating gardens that are both productive and sustainable. By understanding the roles different plants play and how they interact, gardeners can create thriving ecosystems that work in harmony rather than requiring constant intervention.

Companion planting is rooted in the idea that plants can support each other in a multitude of ways. Some partnerships are based on physical protection. For instance, taller plants can provide shade for more delicate crops that might otherwise struggle in direct sunlight. Corn and beans are a classic example of this principle. Corn grows tall and sturdy, creating a natural trellis for bean vines to climb. In return, the beans fix nitrogen in the soil, enriching it for the corn and other plants growing nearby. This mutual exchange exemplifies the balance that can be achieved when plants are paired thoughtfully.

Other plants act as natural repellents for pests, safeguarding their neighbors from potential damage. Marigolds, with their bright flowers and pungent scent, are famous for deterring nematodes and other harmful insects. When planted alongside vegetables like tomatoes or peppers, they create a protective barrier that reduces the need for chemical pesticides. Similarly, aromatic herbs such as basil, rosemary, and thyme can confuse or repel pests with their strong scents, providing a shield for more vulnerable crops. These natural defenses allow gardeners to maintain healthy plants while supporting beneficial insects like bees and butterflies.

Some companions improve soil conditions, making it more fertile and better suited for growth. Legumes such as peas, beans, and clover are particularly valuable in this regard. Through their symbiotic relationship with nitrogen-fixing bacteria, they convert atmospheric nitrogen into forms that plants can absorb, enriching the soil for future crops. This process is especially beneficial in crop rotations, where nitrogen-hungry plants like corn or leafy greens follow legumes in the planting sequence. Cover crops, too, can act as companions by suppressing weeds, reducing erosion, and adding organic matter to the soil when turned under.

Trap cropping is another strategy within companion planting, where one plant is used to lure pests away from a more valuable crop. Nasturtiums, for example, attract aphids, effectively drawing them away from vegetables like lettuce or cabbage. By sacrificing a small portion of the garden to these "decoy" plants, gardeners can protect their main harvest without resorting to harmful chemicals. This method not only preserves the integrity of the primary crop but also supports the broader ecosystem by providing food for beneficial predators like ladybugs and lacewings.

Timing also plays a crucial role in companion planting. Some plants have growth cycles that complement one another, allowing them to share space efficiently. Fast-growing radishes, for instance, can be planted alongside slower-growing carrots. The radishes mature quickly and can be harvested early, leaving room for the carrots to develop without competition. This approach maximizes productivity in limited spaces, making it ideal for small gardens or intensive farming systems.

Beyond these practical benefits, companion planting enhances biodiversity, creating a garden that mimics the complexity of natural ecosystems. A diverse planting scheme attracts a wider range of pollinators and predators, fostering a balanced environment where no single species dominates. This diversity reduces the risk of pest outbreaks and diseases, as a variety of plants and insects create natural checks and balances. A garden rich in different textures, colors, and scents is not only healthier but also more visually appealing, drawing the eye as well as supporting the land.

One of the most well-known examples of companion planting comes from Indigenous agricultural traditions in the Americas, where the "Three Sisters" method has been practiced for centuries. Corn, beans, and squash are planted together, each fulfilling a specific role. The corn provides a structure for the beans to climb, the beans fix nitrogen in the soil, and the sprawling squash vines act as a living mulch, suppressing weeds and retaining moisture. This ingenious system demonstrates how thoughtful combinations can yield abundant harvests while nurturing the soil.

However, companion planting is not without its challenges. Not all plants get along, and some combinations can hinder growth rather than promote it. For instance, onions and beans are poor companions, as onions release compounds that can stifle the growth of legumes. Similarly, plants with similar nutrient needs may compete rather than collaborate, depleting the soil and reducing yields. Successful companion planting requires careful planning and observation, as well as an understanding of the specific needs and behaviors of each plant.

Over time, gardeners develop a deeper sense of how their plants interact, refining their strategies to suit the unique conditions of their soil, climate, and crops. Keeping a garden journal to track the successes and failures of different pairings can be invaluable, providing insights that improve results year after year. Experimentation is part of the process, as no two gardens are exactly alike, and what works in one location may need adjustment in another.

The principles of companion planting extend beyond the vegetable patch, offering lessons in balance, cooperation, and sustainability that apply to all areas of life. By observing how plants support one another and learning from their interactions, gardeners can cultivate not just healthier gardens but also a deeper connection to the natural world. These partnerships remind us that growth is rarely a solitary endeavor; it is the result of relationships, both seen and unseen, that enable life to flourish.

Companion planting offers a way to work with nature rather than against it, creating gardens that are resilient, productive, and beautiful. It celebrates the diversity and interdependence of the plant kingdom, showing us that even the smallest collaborations can yield remarkable results. By embracing these strategies, gardeners can transform their spaces into thriving ecosystems, where every plant plays a part in the success of the whole. Through thoughtful planning and care, companion planting becomes more than a technique—it becomes a philosophy, a way of seeing the garden as a community rather than a collection of individual parts.

Succession Planning

Succession planning is a natural process that governs ecosystems, shaping how plant communities evolve over time. It is the gradual and systematic transition of species within an area, driven by environmental factors, competition, and the natural lifecycle of plants and organisms. By understanding this concept, gardeners, farmers, and land managers can work alongside nature to create landscapes that are resilient, sustainable, and productive. It's not just about managing the present; it's about anticipating the future and fostering conditions that allow ecosystems to thrive long after initial planting.

In its essence, ecological succession begins with a blank canvas. This could be a barren landscape, a recently cleared patch of land, or soil left bare after a disturbance such as fire, flood, or human activity. Nature wastes no time in reclaiming these spaces. The first stage, known as primary succession, occurs when life begins to establish itself in areas previously devoid of soil, like volcanic rock or glacial deposits. In these situations, pioneer species step in—plants that are hardy, adaptable, and capable of surviving in extreme conditions. Mosses, lichens, and certain grasses are examples of pioneers that begin the process of breaking down rock into the first layers of soil, creating the foundation for future growth.

Secondary succession, on the other hand, takes place in areas where soil already exists but has been disturbed. This type happens more quickly because the groundwork has already been laid. For instance, a field left fallow after farming or a forest recovering from a fire are examples of secondary succession. In these contexts, weeds and fast-growing plants are often the first to emerge. These species, sometimes labeled as opportunistic, are not permanent residents. Instead, they act as placeholders, stabilizing the environment and preparing it for more complex communities to follow.

The role of pioneer species in succession planning is not just to occupy space but to transform it. Their roots anchor soil, preventing erosion, while their decomposition enriches it with organic matter. Over time, these early plants change the physical and chemical properties of the soil, making it more hospitable for other species. Gradually, shrubs and perennials take hold, their deeper root systems reaching nutrients beyond the reach of annual pioneers. This progression continues until the climax community is established—a stable, mature ecosystem suited to the local environment. In forests, this might mean towering trees like oaks or pines. In grasslands, it could be a dense mix of perennial grasses and flowering plants.

Succession is not a linear or predictable process, as many factors influence the direction it takes. Soil composition, water availability, climate, and even the presence of animals can alter the trajectory. For example, in an area where grazing animals are prevalent, grasses and low-growing plants may dominate for extended periods instead of giving way to shrubs or trees. Similarly, invasive species can disrupt natural succession by outcompeting native plants, changing the ecosystem's balance.

For anyone managing land, succession planning is both a challenge and an opportunity. By observing how natural succession unfolds, it is possible to guide the process in a way that aligns with specific goals. For instance, in agriculture, cover crops can be used to mimic the early stages of succession, protecting soil and adding nutrients between planting cycles. Choosing the right cover crop—whether it's legumes to fix nitrogen or grasses to prevent erosion—depends on the long-term needs of the land. Farmers who understand succession can rotate crops in a way that maintains soil fertility, reduces pest pressures, and maximizes yield over time.

In reforestation or habitat restoration, succession planning becomes even more critical. Planting pioneer species first, such as hardy shrubs or fast-growing trees, creates the conditions for more sensitive or slow-growing species to succeed later. These pioneers provide shade, reduce wind exposure, and improve soil structure, all of which are essential for supporting the next wave of growth. Over time, as the pioneers fulfill their role, they give way to mid-succession species and, eventually, the climax community. This layered approach not only accelerates recovery but also ensures long-term stability.

Succession planning also plays a role in garden design, particularly in spaces designed to evolve over time. Perennials, shrubs, and trees require patience, as they take years to reach their full potential. Pairing these slower-growing plants with annuals or fast-maturing species ensures that the garden remains vibrant and functional throughout the transitional years. For instance, while a young orchard may take a decade to produce significant fruit, planting fast-growing vegetables or flowers between the trees provides immediate benefits, both aesthetically and nutritionally. As the orchard matures, these temporary plants can be phased out, allowing the trees to take center stage.

While succession planning often feels like a future-focused endeavor, it is equally about observing and responding to the present. Nature provides constant feedback, revealing what works and what doesn't. A patch of soil that remains bare despite planting may need additional organic matter or protection from wind. A species that thrives unexpectedly might signal a shift in the local ecosystem, such as changes in water availability or soil pH. By staying attuned to these signals, it becomes possible to adjust plans and guide succession in a way that aligns with both the land's needs and your vision for it.

The beauty of succession planning lies in its adaptability. It embraces change as an inherent part of growth, recognizing that ecosystems are not static but dynamic. This mindset encourages patience and long-term thinking, qualities that are often at odds with the urgency of modern agriculture or landscaping. Yet, by working with succession rather than against it, the results are more sustainable and enduring.

Every landscape tells a story of succession, from the first weeds pushing through cracks in the pavement to the ancient forests that have stood for centuries. These stories remind us that growth is a process, one that requires time, nurturing, and a willingness to adapt. By incorporating the principles of succession planning into our stewardship of the land, we not only honor nature's rhythms but also ensure that the ecosystems we cultivate today will continue to flourish for generations to come.

Chapter 7: Sustainable Harvest and Regeneration

Timing Your Harvest

The timing of a harvest is as much an art as it is a science. Each crop has its own rhythm, a subtle set of cues that signal the moment when flavor, nutrition, and yield align perfectly. Harvesting too early can mean sacrificing taste and quality, while waiting too long risks overripeness, spoilage, or loss to pests and weather. For anyone who grows their own food—whether in a backyard garden, a small farm, or larger agricultural operations—the ability to observe, interpret, and act on these natural signals is an invaluable skill.

Crops mature according to their life cycles, which are influenced by factors such as temperature, sunlight, soil conditions, and the variety chosen. Some plants, like leafy greens, are harvested at their peak tenderness, while others, such as root vegetables, require time to develop the full depth of flavor below the surface. Fruits often have their own peculiarities, with some ripening on the plant and others continuing to mature after being picked. Knowing the particular needs and characteristics of each crop is the first step in mastering the timing of harvests.

The visual appearance of a plant often provides the most immediate clues about its readiness for harvest. The color of fruits and vegetables is a primary indicator, as they often change hues when they reach peak ripeness. Tomatoes, for example, transition from green to a deep red or golden yellow, depending on the variety. Similarly, the vibrant orange of a carrot or the creamy white of a cauliflower signals that the vegetable has reached its prime. However, color alone is not always enough. Some crops, like watermelons, require a closer look. The underside of the fruit, where it rests on the ground, reveals a creamy yellow spot when ripe, a subtle indicator that experienced growers know to check.

Texture is another key factor in determining harvest timing. The firmness of a fruit or vegetable can signal whether it is ready to be picked. A ripe peach gives slightly under gentle pressure, striking the perfect balance between firmness and juiciness. On the other hand, a cucumber or zucchini should feel firm and smooth, with no soft spots that could indicate overripeness. For grains and seeds, texture often provides an equally important signal. Wheat, for instance, is harvested when the kernels are hard and dry, ensuring the highest quality for storage and milling.

Flavor and aroma are perhaps the most rewarding indicators of harvest readiness. Tasting a cherry tomato, nibbling on a leaf of basil, or inhaling the fragrance of a ripe strawberry can reveal more than any visual or tactile inspection. These sensory cues are especially important for crops like herbs, where essential oils peak at specific stages of growth. Timing the harvest for herbs in the early morning, when dew has evaporated but before the sun's heat diminishes their oils, ensures maximum flavor and potency.

Environmental factors also play a crucial role in harvest timing, particularly for crops sensitive to weather conditions. Rain, for example, can swell fruits and vegetables with water, diluting their flavor and making them more prone to splitting or rot. In the case of grapes destined for winemaking, rainfall close to harvest can drastically alter the sugar content and acidity, affecting the balance of the final product. Similarly, frost can damage crops like tomatoes and peppers, making it essential to harvest them before cold temperatures set in. Understanding the local climate and keeping a close eye on weather patterns allows growers to anticipate these challenges and adapt their harvesting schedules accordingly.

The timing of a harvest doesn't only affect the quality of the food; it also plays a role in the plant's overall health and productivity. For crops that can produce multiple harvests, such as lettuce, beans, or zucchini, picking regularly encourages continued growth and prevents plants from going to seed prematurely. Allowing a plant to mature beyond its ideal window can signal the end of its productive cycle, as it shifts its energy from producing edible parts to focusing on reproduction. Regular harvesting ensures a steady supply of fresh produce while maintaining the vitality of the plant.

Storage considerations are another important factor in timing a harvest. Some crops, like potatoes and winter squash, benefit from being left in the ground or on the vine to cure, a process that hardens their skins and extends their shelf life. Others, such as sweet corn, should be harvested as close to the moment of consumption as possible, as their sugars begin converting to starch immediately after picking, diminishing their sweetness. Planning ahead for how and when crops will be consumed or stored helps to determine the optimal harvest time.

Timing the harvest becomes even more complex in larger-scale operations where multiple crops are grown simultaneously. In these cases, careful planning and coordination are crucial to avoid missing the narrow windows of opportunity for each crop. Many farmers rely on tools like growing degree days—a measure of heat accumulation during the growing season—to predict the maturation of crops. Combining this data with hands-on observation allows for a more precise harvest schedule, ensuring that crops are picked at their peak.

The human element of harvesting is just as critical as the natural cues provided by the plants. An attentive grower develops an intuitive sense for timing, honed by years of experience and observation. This intuition often bridges the gap between scientific knowledge and the unpredictable realities of nature. A farmer might notice the subtle shine on a blueberry that signals ripeness or feel the slight give in a butternut squash that says it's ready for storage. These skills, passed down through generations or learned through trial and error, are what transform harvesting from a task into a craft.

The culmination of months of planting, tending, and waiting, the act of harvesting is both a celebration and a responsibility. The timing of this moment determines not only the immediate quality of the food but also its impact on the land, the plants, and the grower's future success. To harvest well is to understand the cycles of nature, to listen to the silent language of the plants, and to act with care and precision. When done right, it ensures that the fruits of labor are enjoyed at their very best, a reward for the patience and effort invested throughout the growing season.

Seed Saving Cycles

The practice of seed saving is as old as agriculture itself, a vital tradition passed down through generations that preserves genetic diversity while fostering self-reliance. Long before the advent of modern seed companies, farmers and gardeners carefully selected seeds from their best plants, ensuring the continuity of crops that were perfectly adapted to local climates, soils, and tastes. Today, as the global seed market grows increasingly consolidated, the importance of seed saving cycles has never been greater. By understanding the life cycles of plants and implementing thoughtful strategies for seed collection, growers can maintain resilient, productive gardens and contribute to the preservation of biodiversity.

At its core, seed saving begins with observation. Every plant in a garden carries unique characteristics—size, shape, flavor, resistance to disease, or the ability to thrive in particular conditions. Choosing seeds from the plants that best embody desirable traits is the foundation of seed saving. This selection process ensures that future generations of plants will inherit the same strengths, gradually adapting to the specific microclimates and growing conditions of the area. For example, a tomato plant that thrives during an unusually hot and dry season may produce seeds that yield drought-resistant offspring, better equipped to handle similar conditions in the future.

Timing is crucial when it comes to saving seeds. Unlike harvesting fruits or vegetables for consumption, seed collection requires allowing plants to reach full maturity, often beyond the point at which their edible parts are at their peak. For annual crops like tomatoes, peppers, and beans, this means leaving fruits on the plant until they are fully ripe or even overripe. In the case of leafy greens or herbs, it involves letting the plants bolt, or flower, and waiting for the seeds to form and dry. Root crops like carrots and beets, which are biennials, require an extra season to produce seeds, as they do not flower until their second year of growth. Patience is key, as seeds harvested prematurely may not be viable.

The process of collecting seeds varies depending on the type of plant. Dry seeds—such as those from beans, peas, and lettuce—are among the easiest to save. These seeds are enclosed in pods or husks that dry naturally on the plant. Once the pods are fully dry and brittle, they can be harvested and carefully opened to release the seeds. Wet seeds, such as those from tomatoes, cucumbers, and melons, require a bit more effort. These seeds are embedded in the fruit's flesh and are often surrounded by a gelatinous coating that must be removed before storage. Fermentation is a common method for cleaning wet seeds, as it breaks down the protective coating and reduces the risk of disease transmission. After cleaning, the seeds must be thoroughly dried before they can be stored.

Seed storage is as critical as the collection itself. Viability depends on keeping seeds in conditions that are cool, dark, and dry. Moisture, heat, and light can all compromise the longevity of seeds, reducing their ability to germinate. Many gardeners use airtight containers, such as glass jars or resealable bags, to protect seeds from humidity. Labeling is equally important, as it ensures that each seed variety can be identified accurately even months or years later. Including details such as the plant's name, variety, and collection date helps maintain an organized seed library and allows for better planning in future growing seasons.

One of the most significant challenges in seed saving is maintaining the purity of seed varieties. Cross-pollination, which occurs when pollen from one plant fertilizes another, can lead to hybrid seeds that do not reliably produce plants with the same characteristics as their parents. This is particularly common in crops like squash, corn, and peppers, which are prone to cross-pollination due to their reliance on wind or insects for pollination. To preserve the integrity of a seed variety, growers can take steps such as isolating plants by distance, using physical barriers like row covers, or hand-pollinating flowers and bagging them to prevent unintended crosses.

Seed saving also plays a vital role in preserving heirloom varieties, which are open-pollinated plants that have been passed down through generations. These seeds carry unique flavors, colors, and qualities that are often lost in commercial varieties bred for uniformity and shelf stability. By saving and sharing heirloom seeds, gardeners contribute to the conservation of agricultural heritage, ensuring that these distinctive plants remain accessible for future generations. Seed swaps, community seed libraries, and cooperative networks provide opportunities to exchange seeds and knowledge, fostering a sense of connection and shared responsibility among growers.

The cyclical nature of seed saving mirrors the rhythms of the natural world. Each season begins with planting seeds from the previous year's harvest, continuing the legacy of the plants that came before. As the growing season progresses, the cycle comes full circle with the collection of new seeds, ready to be stored and sown again. This continuity is a reminder of the interconnectedness between humans and the earth, a partnership that sustains life and ensures the survival of diverse species.

In modern times, the practice of seed saving carries an added layer of significance. As industrial agriculture prioritizes uniformity and control, the genetic diversity of crops is increasingly at risk. Many traditional varieties have already been lost, replaced by hybrids and genetically modified seeds that cannot be saved and replanted by farmers. By engaging in seed saving, individuals take an active role in preserving genetic diversity, protecting the adaptability and resilience of crops in the face of climate change, pests, and diseases.

The act of saving seeds is deeply empowering. It places the grower at the center of the food system, reducing dependence on external seed sources and fostering a sense of self-sufficiency. It also cultivates a deeper relationship with plants, as each seed carries the story of its growth, care, and selection. Whether saving seeds from a sprawling pumpkin patch or a single cherished sunflower, the process connects the grower to the cycles of life and the enduring legacy of agriculture.

Seed saving is more than a technique; it is a tradition, a form of resistance, and a commitment to the future. By preserving the seeds of today, growers ensure that the gardens and fields of tomorrow will be as vibrant, diverse, and abundant as those of the past. It is in these cycles, repeated year after year, that the resilience of nature and the ingenuity of humanity find their most enduring expression.

Food Preservation Methods

Preserving food has been an essential human endeavor for thousands of years, born out of necessity to extend the shelf life of harvests and ensure sustenance during times when fresh produce was scarce. From ancient techniques passed down through generations to modern innovations, the methods of food preservation are as diverse as the cultures that developed them. Each method reflects a unique understanding of the natural processes that affect food, harnessing elements like temperature, moisture, and microbial activity to keep ingredients safe, flavorful, and nutritious over time.

Drying is one of the oldest and simplest preservation techniques, used by early civilizations to prolong the usability of fruits, vegetables, meats, and herbs. By removing moisture, the primary factor that enables bacterial and fungal growth, drying effectively halts spoilage while concentrating flavors. Sun drying, a method still widely practiced in many parts of the world, relies on warmth and air circulation to achieve this goal. Imagine rows of tomatoes laid out under the sun in Mediterranean villages or strips of fish and meat hanging in the arid winds of Central Asia. Modern dehydrators and ovens have refined this process, offering consistent results and allowing for preservation even in less-than-ideal climates.

Freezing has revolutionized food preservation, offering a straightforward and highly effective way to maintain freshness. By lowering the temperature to levels where microbial activity and enzymatic reactions are nearly halted, freezing preserves the texture, flavor, and nutritional value of food. The convenience of freezing is unmatched; fruits like berries can be flash-frozen to retain their shape, while soups and stews can be stored for months, ready to provide a taste of home-cooked comfort in an instant. However, not all foods freeze equally well. The high water content in some vegetables, such as cucumbers or lettuce, can lead to textural changes upon thawing, while dairy-based sauces may separate. Understanding these nuances helps optimize the use of freezing as a preservation tool.

Fermentation is a preservation method that not only extends the shelf life of food but also transforms its flavor, texture, and nutritional profile. This ancient practice relies on the activity of beneficial microorganisms—bacteria, yeast, and mold—that produce acids or alcohol as byproducts, creating an environment inhospitable to harmful microbes. Each culture has its signature fermented foods, from sauerkraut and kimchi to yogurt, miso, and sourdough bread. Beyond preservation, fermentation enriches foods with probiotics, promoting gut health and enhancing digestibility. It's a process that requires patience and careful monitoring, as temperature, salinity, and time must align to achieve the desired results.

Canning emerged as a groundbreaking innovation in the early 19th century, providing a reliable way to store food for long periods without refrigeration. The process involves sealing food in airtight containers and heating them to destroy spoilage-causing microorganisms. Pressure canning is essential for low-acid foods like meats and vegetables, while water bath canning suffices for high-acid foods such as fruits, jams, and pickles. The vacuum-sealed environment created during canning prevents recontamination, allowing for storage that spans months or even years. While canning demands meticulous attention to sterilization and technique, the rewards are substantial—homemade preserves, sauces, and stocks that retain their quality and flavor far beyond their growing season.

Pickling, another method steeped in history, combines the preservation power of acid and salt. By submerging vegetables, fruits, or even meats in a solution of vinegar or brine, pickling creates an environment that inhibits bacterial growth while infusing the food with sharp, tangy flavors. Dill pickles, olives, and sauerkraut are classic examples, but the art of pickling extends far beyond these staples. In parts of Asia, pickled mangoes and lemons are cherished delicacies, while Scandinavian traditions include pickled herring. The versatility of pickling makes it a favorite among home preservers, allowing for endless experimentation with spices, herbs, and flavor profiles.

Vacuum sealing has become a popular preservation method in recent decades, offering a modern solution to the age-old challenge of keeping food fresh. By removing air from packaging, vacuum sealing minimizes oxidation and slows the growth of aerobic bacteria and mold. This technique pairs exceptionally well with freezing, as it prevents freezer burn and extends storage life. Additionally, vacuum sealing is invaluable for sous vide cooking, enabling precise temperature control for tender, flavorful results. The compact, airtight nature of vacuum-sealed packages also makes them ideal for organizing and storing bulk purchases, reducing food waste and maximizing efficiency in the kitchen.

Smoking, a method as ancient as drying, imparts a rich, complex flavor to foods while preserving them through the antimicrobial properties of smoke compounds. Traditionally used for meats and fish, smoking involves exposing the food to low heat and aromatic wood smoke over an extended period. Cold smoking, which preserves without cooking, is often used for delicacies like smoked salmon, while hot smoking combines cooking and preservation, producing robust flavors in items like barbecue ribs.

As with other methods, the success of smoking relies on a balance of technique, timing, and the choice of wood, each of which contributes to the final product's character.

Salting, or curing, relies on the dehydrating power of salt to draw moisture out of food, creating an environment hostile to bacteria. This method has roots in nearly every culture, from salted cod in Portugal to prosciutto in Italy and biltong in South Africa. Salt-curing not only preserves food but also intensifies its flavor, producing culinary treasures that stand the test of time. Sugar curing, often paired with salt, is another variation used for items like hams and smoked salmon. These methods, while simple in concept, require precision to achieve the perfect balance of seasoning and preservation.

Each preservation method carries its own advantages and challenges, but all share a common purpose: to extend the life of food while maintaining its quality. By combining methods, such as freezing vacuum-sealed fruits or fermenting vegetables before canning, growers and cooks can tailor preservation strategies to suit their needs and resources. The choice of method often depends on the type of food, the desired outcome, and personal preferences, but the ultimate goal remains the same—to make the harvest last, ensuring nourishment and enjoyment long after the growing season has ended.

Preserving food is more than a practical skill; it is a bridge between seasons, a way to capture the essence of a moment and carry it forward. Each jar of jam, bundle of dried herbs, or wedge of smoked cheese tells a story of time, place, and care. By embracing these methods, we not only reduce waste and enhance self-sufficiency but also honor the traditions and ingenuity that have sustained humanity for generations. Through preservation, we transform food from a fleeting resource into a lasting treasure.

Garden Regeneration

Soil, plants, and ecosystems all follow cycles of birth, growth, death, and renewal. Garden regeneration is the deliberate act of working with these natural processes to restore vitality to the land after a growing season or period of neglect. It's more than maintenance—it's about healing the soil, reinvigorating plant life, and creating the conditions for a thriving garden that can sustain itself season after season. By understanding how to repair and rebuild the essential components of a garden, growers can ensure its health and productivity for years to come.

The foundation of any garden lies in its soil, and regeneration begins with restoring its structure and fertility. Over time, planting and harvesting deplete the nutrients that plants draw on to grow, leaving the soil tired and unbalanced. Compaction from foot traffic, heavy machinery, or even the weight of plants themselves can make it difficult for roots to penetrate the ground and for water and air to circulate. Soil health is deeply tied to its organic matter content, which provides food for microorganisms and improves its ability to hold moisture. Adding compost is one of the most effective ways to replenish organic matter. Made from decomposed plant materials, kitchen scraps, and yard waste, compost reintroduces essential nutrients like nitrogen, phosphorus, and potassium while also fostering the microbial life that turns soil into a living ecosystem.

Cover crops, often called green manures, are another key strategy for garden regeneration. Plants like clover, vetch, and rye are sown not for harvest but to benefit the soil. Their roots hold the soil together and prevent erosion, while their foliage provides a protective cover that reduces water loss and suppresses weeds. When tilled into the soil, these plants release nutrients as they decompose, enriching the ground for the next planting cycle. Legumes, in particular, are valuable because of their ability to fix atmospheric nitrogen, converting it into a form that plants can readily absorb. Growing a cover crop during the offseason ensures that the soil is not left bare and vulnerable while it naturally recovers.

Regeneration also involves addressing soil imbalances that may have built up over time. Testing the soil provides insight into its pH levels, nutrient content, and overall health. If the soil is too acidic or too alkaline, it can limit the availability of nutrients, leading to poor plant growth. Amendments like lime or sulfur can correct pH, while deficiencies can be addressed with specific minerals or organic fertilizers. However, the goal is not to rely on quick fixes but to build a soil ecosystem that supports itself through natural cycles. Mulching is one method that contributes to this balance, as it conserves moisture, moderates soil temperature, and slowly adds organic matter as it breaks down.

Regenerating a garden also means fostering biodiversity, both above and below the soil. Monoculture planting—focusing on a single crop—can exhaust the soil and make it more susceptible to pests and diseases. Planting a diverse range of crops, flowers, and herbs improves soil health by encouraging different root structures and microbial communities. Diverse plantings also attract beneficial insects like pollinators and predators that keep pest populations in check. Adding native plants to the garden strengthens local ecosystems, providing habitat and food for birds, bees, and butterflies that play essential roles in maintaining balance.

Pruning and removing dead plant material are another important part of regeneration. While some organic matter can be left to decompose naturally, excessive debris from diseased or pest-ridden plants should be removed and destroyed to prevent further spread. Cutting back perennials and shrubs encourages healthy new growth in the next season, while also improving air circulation and reducing the risk of fungal diseases. At the same time, leaving certain plants, like sunflowers or ornamental grasses, standing through the winter can provide shelter and food for wildlife, contributing to the garden's ecological health.

Water management is a critical component of regeneration, particularly in areas prone to drought or heavy rainfall. Overwatering can compact soil and wash away nutrients, while insufficient moisture can stress plants and reduce microbial activity. Techniques like drip irrigation and rainwater harvesting help regulate water use, ensuring it is delivered efficiently and sustainably. In addition, improving soil structure through organic matter and mulching increases its ability to retain water, reducing the need for supplemental watering.

Pest and disease management are often overlooked as part of garden regeneration, but they are integral to restoring balance. Chemical pesticides and herbicides may offer quick solutions, but they often disrupt the natural systems that keep pests and diseases in check. Encouraging natural predators, such as ladybugs, lacewings, and birds, helps control pest populations without the need for harmful chemicals. Crop rotation is another effective strategy, as it prevents pests and diseases from becoming established by disrupting their life cycles. For example, planting brassicas in one area one year and legumes the next breaks the chain of pests and pathogens that target specific crops.

The role of the gardener in this process is not just to intervene but to observe and collaborate with nature. A regenerated garden is one that works in harmony with its environment, rather than against it. By paying attention to the needs of the soil, plants, and animals that share the space, gardeners can make informed decisions that benefit the entire ecosystem. For instance, rather than clearing every fallen leaf, allowing some to remain creates a natural mulch that enriches the soil and provides habitat for insects and other small creatures.

Regeneration is not a one-time task but an ongoing commitment. Each season offers an opportunity to learn from the successes and challenges of the past and to refine practices for the future. Over time, these efforts create a garden that is not only productive but resilient, capable of withstanding the stresses of changing weather patterns, pests, and diseases. A well-regenerated garden is more than the sum of its parts—it is a living, breathing system that supports itself and its surroundings.

Every act of regeneration is an investment in the future. By renewing the soil, encouraging biodiversity, and restoring balance, gardeners create spaces that are not only beautiful and bountiful but also sustainable. These gardens become places of renewal not just for the land but for the people who tend them, offering the satisfaction of working with nature to create something enduring. In regeneration, the garden and the gardener grow together, each becoming stronger, healthier, and more deeply connected to the cycles of life.

Creating Perpetual Systems

Perpetual systems in gardening and farming are designed to sustain themselves over time, reducing the need for constant human intervention while maintaining balance, productivity, and ecological health. The concept draws heavily from observing natural ecosystems, where resources cycle continuously, waste becomes a source of nourishment, and every element serves a purpose. By mimicking these principles, growers can create systems that are not only efficient but also resilient in the face of environmental challenges.

At the heart of a perpetual system lies the idea of closed loops—cycles in which outputs from one process become inputs for another. Organic matter, for example, is never discarded but instead transformed into compost, which enriches the soil and feeds the next generation of plants. This cycle mirrors what happens in a forest, where fallen leaves and dead plants decompose, returning nutrients to the earth and supporting new growth. Composting is the cornerstone of any sustainable garden, converting kitchen scraps, garden clippings, and other biodegradable materials into a rich, fertile amendment that not only improves soil structure but also fosters microbial life. These microorganisms, in turn, break down organic matter further, making nutrients available to plants in a form they can absorb.

Water management is another key element of perpetual systems, as it ensures that this vital resource is used wisely and efficiently. Rainwater harvesting represents one of the simplest yet most effective ways to create a sustainable water loop. By collecting rainwater in barrels or cisterns, growers can reduce their reliance on municipal water supplies while ensuring a steady source of water during dry periods. Pairing rainwater collection with irrigation systems like drip lines or soaker hoses maximizes efficiency, delivering water directly to the roots where it is needed most. Beyond collection, the design of the garden itself plays a role in water sustainability. Contour planting, where crops are arranged to follow the natural curves of the land, helps slow runoff and encourages water infiltration into the soil. Mulching further aids this process by retaining soil moisture, reducing evaporation, and moderating temperatures around plant roots.

Diversity is a hallmark of natural ecosystems and a critical component of perpetual systems. In monoculture setups, where single crops dominate, the risk of pest outbreaks and nutrient depletion is high. Diverse plantings, on the other hand, mimic the complexity of nature, creating an environment where different species support one another. Companion planting is a practice that leverages these relationships, pairing plants that benefit each other in various ways. For instance, marigolds are often planted alongside vegetables to deter harmful insects, while legumes like beans enrich the soil with nitrogen that neighboring plants can use. Polyculture, which involves growing multiple crops in the same space, helps to break pest and disease cycles, improve soil health, and maximize yields. The integration of perennial plants—those that return year after year without the need for replanting—adds another layer of stability, as their deep root systems anchor soil and draw nutrients from deeper layers, making them available to surrounding plants.

The role of animals in perpetual systems cannot be overlooked. In traditional farming, livestock and poultry are often integrated into the system, contributing to its sustainability in multiple ways. Chickens, for instance, provide eggs and meat while also serving as natural pest controllers, feeding on insects and weeds that might otherwise harm crops. Their manure, rich in nutrients like nitrogen and phosphorus, becomes a valuable fertilizer when properly composted. Similarly, grazing animals like sheep or goats can help manage overgrowth in pastures or orchards while also contributing to soil health through their droppings. Even in smaller garden settings, insects such as bees and butterflies play a critical role as pollinators, ensuring the reproduction of fruits, vegetables, and flowers. Attracting these beneficial creatures with native plants, wildflowers, and habitat features like bee hotels or shallow water sources strengthens the system as a whole.

Energy efficiency is another consideration in creating perpetual systems. The use of renewable energy sources, such as solar panels to power irrigation pumps or wind turbines to generate electricity, reduces reliance on fossil fuels and minimizes the system's environmental footprint. On a smaller scale, passive solar techniques—like orienting greenhouses to capture maximum sunlight or using thermal mass materials to store heat—help regulate temperatures and extend the growing season without additional energy inputs. These approaches align with the broader goal of perpetual systems: to work with natural forces rather than against them.

One of the most profound aspects of a perpetual system is its ability to adapt and evolve over time. Unlike static designs, these systems are dynamic, responding to changes in climate, soil conditions, and the needs of the grower. For instance, crop rotation is a practice that prevents nutrient depletion and reduces the buildup of pests and diseases by changing the types of plants grown in a particular area each season. By alternating between crops with different nutrient requirements and growth habits, growers can maintain soil fertility and disrupt pest life cycles. Similarly, observing how plants perform in different conditions allows for adjustments in planting strategies, ensuring that the system remains productive and balanced.

Waste is virtually eliminated in a well-designed perpetual system, as every byproduct finds a purpose. Pruned branches and fallen leaves become mulch or compost, while kitchen scraps are transformed into nutrient-rich soil amendments. Even wastewater from household activities, when properly treated or filtered, can be reused for irrigation in a practice known as greywater recycling. This mindset of using all available resources not only reduces environmental impact but also fosters a deeper connection to the land and its processes.

Perpetual systems are not confined to rural farms or large tracts of land; they can be implemented on any scale, from urban balconies to suburban backyards. In cities, vertical gardening and rooftop farming make efficient use of limited space, while community gardens bring people together to create shared systems that benefit entire neighborhoods. The principles remain the same regardless of size: close the loops, work with nature, and prioritize sustainability.

The success of these systems depends on the grower's ability to observe, learn, and adapt. Nature is the ultimate teacher, offering countless examples of how cycles sustain life without waste or imbalance. By tuning into these lessons and applying them thoughtfully, it's possible to create systems that not only feed and sustain us but also regenerate the land and nurture the ecosystems that depend on it. A perpetual system is a living, breathing entity, one that evolves and thrives through the harmonious collaboration of plants, animals, and humans, ensuring that the cycles of life continue uninterrupted.